What people are saying about *Social Justice Education*...

"Whether you are a seasoned activist or only beginning your journey, you will find something to ignite your passions in this book. Blair Niblett takes the reader on a journey of activism that offers an entry point for all."
—**Mandi Hardy, Middle School Teacher, Peel District School Board**

"Blair Niblett promises readers will feel refueled by this volume. He delivers much-needed refreshment for educators who think critically and yearn for more tools to address privilege and oppression in their classrooms."
—**Leigh Potvin, Ph.D., Department of Communities and Connections, Cape Breton University**

"Niblett has created mandatory reading for every educator! This book truly opens the door to social justice through captivating narratives and real life examples that stir your creativity. Moreover, it explores how education can be activism. Teachers can make learning truly experiential, bringing in real world challenges for which youth can develop solutions. I truly believe it will help youth find how to be themselves and be empowered in their community."
—**Mr. Jeremy Dias, votre directeur général | your Executive Director, Le Centre canadien de la diversité des genres & de la sexualité | The Canadian Centre for Gender & Sexual Diversity**

"The issue of social justice in the classroom has always been a matter in which I tread lightly. As many of my contemporaries, I was taught that neutrality is best when it comes to provocative and controversial issues. Niblett, however, is reassuring in his stance that the classroom can be the best environment for these types of things, so long as that environment is one where respect is established and trust maintained. Moreover, a refusal to address such issues in the classroom serves as a tacit approval of the status quo, and teachers have the responsibility to show students they are capable of being agents of change. Thanks to *Social Justice Education*, tomorrow I can re-enter my school's classrooms knowing that world-changers are all around me, and I have the honor of changing it alongside them."
—**Amy Brewer, Director of Education, Positive Tomorrows**

"Blair Niblett's cogent and candid book brings social justice and activism out of the shadows of education and into the place it belongs in the classroom, where all are invited not as audience but as agents of positive and humane change. Niblett creates a framework for developing a container in which the classroom community can safely share, debate, and practice both critical thinking and humility. In the social justice classroom, learners are trusted to drive their learning process, developing qualities and skills for living in an increasingly diverse world. As education in North America begins to move away from failed reforms like standardization, high-stakes testing and direct instruction, this book is a go-to resource for the dawn of a new progressive era in education.

—Laurie Frank, Experiential Educator, author of *Journey Toward the Caring Classroom, 2 Edition*

SOCIAL JUSTICE EDUCATION

Stories and Strategies for Teachers

SOCIAL JUSTICE EDUCATION

Stories and Strategies for Teachers

Blair Niblett, Ph.D.

Wood N Barnes Publishing
2309 N. Willow, Suite A, Bethany, OK
800.678.0621

1st Edition © 2017, Blair Niblett and Wood N Barnes Publishing, U.S.A.
All rights reserved.

This publication is sold with the understanding that the publisher is not engaged in rendering psychological, medical, or other professional services.

Interior & cover design by Ramona Cunningham

Printed in the United States of America
ISBN 978-1-939019-23-3

This book is dedicated to social justice educators everywhere!
Especially those who gave their valuable time to interviews
that led to the development of this book. 🔘

CONTENTS

INTRODUCTION

Who Should Read This Book?

Teaching and learning are a messy business, for all teachers and all learners. But, educators and learners who are interested in social justice issues often navigate a terrain messier than usual as they integrate equity issues into their everyday work. Many modern school systems in North America operate on the assumption that schools are value-neutral places whose purpose is to focus on reading, writing, and arithmetic—just the facts! Most teachers and many students know, however, that values are an integral part of reading, writing, math, and other school subjects. In fact, some teachers and learners would say values are a fundamental part of what it means to teach and learn, and often those values bump up against issues of justice. Who should be included? How should resources be distributed? Is equal really fair? How should decisions be made when there isn't agreement about answers to these important questions? Teachers who are proponents of social justice (and their students!) often encounter these kinds of questions. They may face resistance to incorporating social justice ideas into curriculum. Such resistance can come from school and district level administrators, parents, community groups, and even from other teachers and students. Knowing real tensions exist between anti-oppressive social change and public schooling, where does this leave teachers who feel committed to social justice values and want to enact those values as part of their teaching?

This book has two main purposes. First, it is intended to connect with teachers already doing anti-oppressive social justice work in their practice and offer support and encouragement. Anti-oppressive social justice education is hard work that can feel lonely at times (though, at other times, its rewards are clear and plentiful!). Some of the teachers who I interviewed while researching this book shared with me that despite their strong commitment to education as a vehicle for social justice, they sometimes feel lost or exhausted by the very slow and incremental rate at which social change occurs in schools and societies. This can be true for all teachers, but I believe it is especially the case for social justice educators. For these teachers, this book offers reassurance that their approaches to education as a means of making a fairer world are worthy, even if it is often an uphill climb. In other words, I hope the book provides a refueling stop for committed social justice teachers.

An equal, second purpose of the book is to connect with teachers who may not immediately identify as teachers for social justice, but who are interested in or amiable to the values that social justice education stands for (more on these values soon!). This book serves as an invitation for them to begin to see themselves as social justice educators. It is an opportunity to reflect on their own personal and professional identities and consider ways they might internalize the idea of social justice education and make it a more intentional part of their teaching practice. The invitation is offered in two main ways. First, the book offers educators some language to help describe the aims and goals of social justice and how these contribute to the aims and goals of education. Some educators may be hesitant to call themselves social justice teachers simply because they feel they don't have the right words to describe how they believe education can function as a vehicle for social justice. The development of a language for social justice education may serve teachers' own understanding of their teaching practice and may also serve as tools for explaining social justice education to others. Second, the book provides would-be social justice teachers with possible activities that can be easily implemented in a classroom to kick-start the practice of social justice pedagogy. In this way, the book's purpose is not only to give teachers language for thinking and talking about social justice in their teaching practice, but also possibilities to actually enact their social justice language in practical ways in their everyday teaching. These practical examples will come in the form of activities and exercises that I have explored in my own teaching.

Situating Myself (the Author) in the Book

I hope readers of this book will ask themselves who I am and why I have chosen to write this book. These kinds of questions are central to the critical work that is a mainstay of social justice education. I use the word critical here to mean something like "analytically sceptical"—a very positive thing in terms of all education, but especially so in social justice education because of the need to assess the fairness in relationships among people and systems.

As a learner, I have always operated a little bit "outside of the box." While I've had a lot of success in formal schooling, I've often made it a point to do things differently. In early elementary school during a unit on pioneer life, we were instructed to stitch our own small quilt blocks using evenly-sized squares of different colours (a simple design, easily sewn by young children). The teacher explained all the blocks would be combined into a full size quilt. I looked at the quilting book she had used to show us some different quilt designs, and asked why all our quilt blocks needed to be the same? Couldn't I make mine in a log cabin style, rather than the more standard patchwork style? Reluctantly, the teacher agreed, and showed me how to cut the rectangular patches needed for my chosen design. Although my alternative quilting story isn't an example of radical activism, it does show how I have always wanted or needed to "break the mold" of standard education.

As an educator, educational researcher, and a learner, I identify as an activist for social and ecological justice. It's important to note that I take a very broad understanding of what it can mean to be an activist when I use this term to describe myself. It does not mean that I'm chaining myself to things in school parking lots, or that I attend every rally on every issue related to education (although I do attend some), or that I organize student walkouts (though, I have been supportive of students who have planned such acts of resistance). Sometimes being an activist educator can be as simple as raising my hand to ask a question about something that most others take for granted, designing learning environments that help students speak with their own voices, and/or attempting to create a safe space for students to talk about socially controversial issues in my classes.

The word "activist" has some negative connotations. Activists may be viewed as renegades, fanatics, or fringe members of society. I want to suggest that one needn't be a radical rebel to be considered an activist—indeed, I think there is much room in public schools for teachers, students, and all other stakeholders to rethink what it means to be radical, and why radical teaching might be something worth striving for. In a society where disconnection and disengagement are becoming a seldom questioned norm (Checkoway, 2011; Zyngier, 2008), any act that resists this disconnection can be thought of as activism—particularly when disconnection and disengagement fuel inequity based on a variety of social factors like race, social class, dis/ability, sexual orientation, and so on. Big or small, quiet or loud, any choice that works to resist the dominance of some people over other people is an activist choice. Sometimes these activist choices may be viewed as "just good teaching," and this view would be correct from my perspective. However, I would still consider these choices examples of activism in education if the choice is premised on an intention to make for more equitable learning environments in the short-term—and a more equitable world as the long-term effects of such learning environments ripple outward. Note the word "choices" used here to describe activist education. This is because I think activism in education isn't only about what teachers do, but is also about how we think, and how that thinking impacts the design of learning environments.

While I identify as an activist educator and invite readers to adopt activist educator identities, I stop short of projecting my identity on others as a requirement of social justice education. Whether a teacher identifies as a radical activist or not, there are opportunities for all teachers to help create a more socially just world by considering how the choices they make in their classrooms have the ability to help or hinder students viewing themselves as change makers who are capable of making the world a more socially- and ecologically-just place.

What This Book Can and Cannot Do

As noted above, this book is intended to be a springboard into social justice education, or a refueling stop for those educators who are already on a path of social justice education. In these ways, the book can serve as a catalyst for either starting or continuing work as an activist educator. The book is not intended as a catalog or recipe book for social justice education. Each reader will need to find ways to integrate some or all of the theories and practices of social justice education discussed in these pages into the context of his or her own work. Social justice education is deeply situated in the specific context in which it plays out. Of course, there are some broad principles that help to drive what it can mean to do social justice education, but these principles are lost if they are not adapted to suit the needs of the specific situation in which they are being applied. In the chapters that follow, I outline some broad principles and highlight examples of how some activist educators are taking up those principles in their work, and invite readers to consider ways that these concepts may be useful in their own practices of education.

The Journey Ahead

This book unfolds into five chapters, divided into two parts. Part one presents foundational ideas that support social justice education and sets up the structure for the second part of the book. The chapters in part two take a deeper dive into the three elements of social justice education established in part one. These chapters are driven by stories shared by educators working through social justice education. Readers who are most interested in those stories may choose to jump directly to part two. Others seeking a more theoretical context before arriving at the stories may wish to start at part one and work through.

Part I :: Foundations

Chapter one is an introduction to the idea of social justice education as a progressive movement. Fundamental to social justice education is the idea that education is always political, even if teachers and students do not view themselves as political actors. In this chapter, I explain why it can be a good thing that education is inherently political and how teachers committed to social justice education can engage students in rich learning experiences, preparing them to act as agents for social justice change now and in the future. A key purpose is for readers to see themselves as social justice educators and/or identify places social justice education might fit within their teaching practice.

Chapter two explores three key elements that make up social justice education: Environments, ideas, and actions. **Environments** are the designed places in which education for social justice can take place, including social, natural, and built environments. **Ideas** refer to knowledge developed to help in the movement toward a more socially just world and the thinking tools used to help develop such knowledge. **Actions** are things teachers and learners can do to help bring a more socially just world into reality. It is important to recognize these elements do not operate independently, but are intertwined within the practice of social justice education. This chapter presents a theoretical basis for understanding these elements and prepares readers to explore the teacher practices in part two.

Part II :: Getting to Work

Chapter three, four, and five each take up one of the key ideas introduced in chapter two. In each of these chapters, teachers' stories and sample activities are provided to serve as practical kick-starters for readers' own practices of social justice education.

Chapter three outlines the nature of educational environments that foster effective social justice education. **Chapter four** offers a sense of the kind of ideas that underpin social justice education and shows ways teachers can help such ideas come to life in their classrooms. This "coming to life" of ideas is extended in **Chapter five**, which looks at the possibilities and pitfalls of social justice actions situated within education.

Chapter six serves as an Outroduction—something more than a summary but less than a conclusion. This is because the end of a book on social justice education is not a conclusion but actually a new beginning for readers who want to make social justice education a part of their teaching or continue doing so with renewed commitment.

PART I FOUNDATIONS

I think that we have to create in ourselves, through critical analysis of our practice, some qualities, some virtues as educators. One of them, for example, is the quality of becoming more and more open to feel the feelings of others, to become so sensitive that we can guess what the group or one person is thinking at that moment.

Paulo Freire

CHAPTER
1

WHAT IS SOCIAL JUSTICE EDUCATION?

Social justice education is not a class nor subject area to be taught, a textbook, a method of assessment, nor a new initiative in the dizzying array of initiatives to which teachers are frequently asked to give their time and attention. Social justice education might have something to say about all of these things, but it cannot be boxed into just one of them. In fact, attempts at packaging social justice education as any one of these tends to hinder its goals of creating schools, communities, and societies that are fairer to all people, all creatures, and the planet we share together.

Social justice education is best understood as a perspective on education held in partnership between teachers and learners about what it means to teach and learn in ways that help individuals be and understand themselves and be in relationship with others in ways that honor principles of social justice. These principles include, but are not limited to: **equity, challenging privilege and oppression, building community, and fostering agency and action**. Two points deserve clarification before some explanation of these principles.

First, the conceptualization of social justice education as a partnership between teachers and learners is paramount. It would be unfair to suggest this is always an equally balanced partnership; however, social justice education will falter if it is something done to students by teachers rather than a process teachers and students join in together. This is to say, at the level of education, social justice values should not be mandated. Those who believe in them must promote the virtues of commitment to social justice principles. While most educational organizations do reasonably mandate particular kinds of pro-social behaviours (e.g., no hitting, no name calling), social justice education must go beyond managing behaviours and invite teachers and learners to consider and adopt underlying values and attitudes that justify such behaviours (Purkey & Novak, 2008). As such, educators cannot rightly demand people think in particular ways. Instead, social justice educators must design engaging experiences, providing students with opportunities to understand the benefits of social justice. If students and teachers take up social justice viewpoints, it should be because they have been given opportunities to consider how to think about what justice and fairness look like, not because they have been taught what to think. This kind of programming must be delivered with generosity. In other words, students must not be enticed to adopt social justice perspectives through threats of exclusion or other punishment. Even those who may be difficult to reach or convince cannot be forced into social justice. When teachers are successful in creating invitations to social justice, they are accessing what some philosophers and brain scientists consider an underlying human sense of empathy. Jeremy Rifkin (2009) describes the educational significance of a human tendency to be concerned for others: "The traditional assumption that 'knowledge is power' and is used for personal gain is being subsumed by the notion that knowledge is the expression of the shared responsibility for the collective well-being of humanity and the planet as a whole" (¶ 42). This changing view of the status of knowledge and learning is a beacon of the need for more and better pedagogies, allowing students and teachers opportunities to translate empathic ideas into social justice actions.

A second related point is that social justice education is fundamentally about relationships among people and the world we inhabit together. There are social, political, and pedagogical elements that need to be attended to as teachers and students engage in teaching and learning together. While all of these elements are important, I draw readers' attention specifically to the social aspect of social justice education, as I believe it has a fundamental significance through which political and pedagogical elements can be understood. Approaching the teaching of political ideas through a social lens allows for a filtering of the sometimes divisive elements of politics and emphasizes the importance of our shared humanity. Modern cultural assumptions about activism place

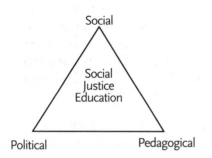

significant emphasis on its political elements. Although most of the teachers I interviewed in conducting the research that led to this book acknowledged each of the social, political, and pedagogical elements that contribute to social justice education, many of them function as social justice educators primarily through a social and/or pedagogical lens. In other words, the social aspect of how participants in a learning community relate influences what they do together to promote social justice more than the commonly understood political dimensions. It must be noted that a social focus does not negate or erase the inherently political nature of social justice work (the social is political!), but emphasizing the social elements of social justice within educational contexts helps to develop environments most conducive to learning.

> **Praxis Point** ✍ Look for "praxis point" sidebars in each chapter of the book. These pit-stops focus the ideas being explored into specific actions or reflective methods educators can implement into their teaching practice (see pages 31 and 39 for more on praxis).

Principles of Social Justice Education

The following principles describe my use of the phrase social justice education throughout the book. These concepts are not an exhaustive or definitive explanation of social justice education, but aim to extend the broader purposes of the book: Supporting educators already identifying as activist educators by offering ideas and examples that resonate with their ongoing practices, as well as inviting more educators to join the broad movement of social justice education by giving them language to describe social justice education and activities that may serve as springboards within their practice. Other authors may include different focus points or place emphasis differently than I do, which I see as a good thing! Diversity is a strength in outlining what doing social justice education can look like, sound like, and feel like. Here, I offer snapshots of the four principles that will be developed throughout the book.

Equity

Equity means that each person in a community can receive what they need in order to participate fully in the life of that community to the fullest extent the teacher, school administration, and wider community can provide.* This may include fair access to resources as well as respectful acknowledgement as a valued member of the community (Cribb & Gewirtz, 2003; Young, 1990). Equity goes beyond equal treatment in recognition that individuals and groups may have different needs that must be respected in order for them to participate fully and meaningfully in social life (Sensoy & DiAngelo, 2012).

Social justice expert Mara Sapon-Shevin (2007) describes inclusion (a corollary of equity) using the metaphor of a dinner party where the host carefully plans the elements of the party (menu, room layout, conversation starters, activities) so each guest and the group as a whole can get the most out of coming to the party. Sapon-Shevin states, "It's within schools that children and adults learn some of the most basic lessons about who matters in the world.... It is only within inclusive schools that anyone can become a fully loving and competent human being. And so... inclusion is good for—even essential to—a thriving democracy" (p. xiii). Sapon-Shevin's idea of inclusion and the notion of equity developed in this book are compatible. While equity may focus more on political aspects of justice such as division of resources and the application of legal protections, inclusionary values set the stage for such discussions. Together, inclusion and equity develop a mindset for teaching and learning in which privilege and oppression can be challenged.

Challenging Privilege and Oppression

Equity gives a name to the main goal of social justice education; however, just naming or describing desired outcomes is only a beginning. Teachers and students who are practitioners of social justice education also actively challenge the social structures and routines that allow inequity to continue (Freire, 1985, 2013; Nieto & Bode, 2012; Smith, Down, & McInerney, 2014).

---

* Here, I recognize that many teachers are committed to creating equitable classrooms, but there may be limiting factors created by shortages of resources or structural/ideological barriers created by systemic inequity that are part of the larger education system of a given community, region, or nation.

Sensoy and DiAngelo (2012) express privilege and oppression as opposite sides of the same coin. They define privilege as "the rights, advantages, and protections enjoyed by some *at the expense of* and beyond the rights, advantages, and protections available to others" (p. 57, emphasis in original). In order for some people to experience privilege, others experience its opposite, oppression—even when the oppression isn't obvious to the person who experiences it or others around them. Oppression is defined as "a set of policies, practices, traditions, norms, definitions, and explanations ... which function to systematically exploit one social group to the benefit of another social group" (p. 39).

Two factors about privilege often go unsaid, and Sensoy & DiAngelo's (2012) definition highlights them. First, privilege is often unearned, and second it is largely inescapable for those who experience it. In other words, some with privilege don't necessarily do anything to become privileged and cannot simply give their privilege away even if they want to. Understanding these factors may be helpful in relieving the feelings of guilt and shame associated with calling someone privileged. This is significant because these negative feelings attached to privilege can lead people to deny or ignore their privileged position, a move which almost certainly strengthens the power difference between experiencing privilege and experiencing oppression. Instead of thinking of privilege as only a negative condition (i.e., a spoiled child), the experience of privilege can be conceived as a positive opportunity, if that privilege is used to distribute social power more equitably. For instance, someone who has the privilege to attend post-secondary education (college or university) may have opportunities to use their privileged social position to benefit others who may not experience the same privilege (more in a moment on spending privilege).

For Sensoy and DiAngelo (2012), the primary factor that mediates privilege and oppression is social power. Teachers hold a certain amount of power by virtue of their position (even though they may experience oppression through other elements of their identity). They have the ability to use this power to maintain relationships of privilege and oppression or to equalize these relationships. The question of how teachers **spend their privilege** (Russell, 2014) and help students to understand privilege and oppression is a key factor in social justice education. The concept of challenging privilege and oppression could be taken up in the sense of aggressive protest, but my research suggests that teachers who identify as social justice educators—at least the ones I spoke to, don't tend to take up social justice in this way in their teaching. Rather, their challenge to privilege and oppression, and the challenge they pose to their students, is for each individual to spend their privilege through actions in everyday life that tend toward equity rather than maintaining privilege and oppression. One means of facilitating an invitation for students to spend their privilege in equitable ways is by developing learning communities that showcase various kinds of equity, in which the classroom community becomes a microcosm of the broader community students and teachers want to build.

Building Community

Development of community is essential to the effective practice of social justice education. Outside of community, social justice becomes an abstract notion where the humanitarian justice it promotes can become lost or misdirected. The heart of social justice organizing lies in **community movements**. Such movements are created when people who have decided they are unwilling to continue living under the negative conditions they are experiencing (racism, sexism, environmental degradation, etc.) link up with others who are also experiencing such oppression or are allied with those who are through their shared humanity (Palmer, 2007).

For teachers who identify as social justice educators, developing an intentional sense of community in the classroom must be a precursor to content learning around sociopolitical issues. It is the safety of community that allows for learning about these most contentious issues in our world and gives individuals and small groups of students the courage to take action to change their world.

Fostering Agency and Action

In discussing the tone of public schooling, author Laurie Frank (2013) suggests "there is a ubiquitous mood in our education system that is uninviting" (p. 14). Often, uninviting school environments are developed through systems and structures that allow and encourage students to take roles almost exclusively as educational consumers rather than contributing partners in their own education (Carr, 2011; Jensen, 2004). This positioning of students leads to the creation of a sense of apathy—a belief on the part of people young and old that their efforts and actions to shape their world don't really make a difference.

Social justice education aims to challenge this belief through the fostering of agency and action.

Designing experiences that engaged learners is key. Palmer (2007) describes an approach to educational design that is neither teacher-centered, nor learner-centered, but subject-centered. As a basic example, Palmer offers kindergarten:

> Watch a good teacher sitting on the floor with a group of five-year-olds, reading a story about an elephant. Viewed through the eyes of those children, it is almost possible to see that elephant in the middle of the circle! And with the "great thing" as the vehicle, other great things come into the room—things like language and the miracle of symbols that carry meaning (pp. 120-121).

Palmer's exemplar shows that in a subject-centered learning environment, the typical face-to-face positioning of teacher and student, where one acts on the other is adjusted, allowing student and teacher to stand side-by-side and study the "great thing," which is the subject of the learning, together. A second meaning also found in Palmer's concept of subject-centered learning is that in the side-by-side orientation, both student and teacher are granted "subjecthood,"—they become purposeful actors in the learning experience rather than objects that are acted upon, which is often the case in traditional approaches to education (Freire, 1970).

Agency is an idea—students' belief in their own value and abilities as community members—that can lead to **action**. Certainly, it is possible for students to engage in action without a belief in their own agency, but in such cases students may not have an understanding of why they are taking particular actions. In the case of social justice actions, this can lead to disingenuous action where students might explain their actions as "because the teacher said." This response either demonstrates a lack of understanding or a state of coercion, both of which are unsatisfactory from a social justice education perspective. The possibility of such a response reinforces the importance of invitation and understanding as foundations of social justice education. Social justice educators seek to develop in students an understanding of principles of social fairness, in which action becomes an extension of deeply held principles. A key word in the phrasing of this principle is **fostering**, which highlights that teachers should not force students into social justice action. Indeed, to be serious about agency as a goal of social justice requires teachers to recognize students as free people who may reject any particular social justice ideas or actions the teacher brings forward. In this way, student agency is both the lifeblood of social justice education and also a factor that makes designing and implementing social justice education a highly complex undertaking. Such complexities are highlighted many times over in the teachers' stories shared later in this book.

Praxis Point 📓 Consider keeping a social justice journal for your teaching practice. Document your observations around the four principles of social justice education presented here, as well as other elements of social justice that are important to you as an educator and/or in the context in which you work. Just include enough description to refresh your memory when reviewed. If you already keep a day planner or other running record (hard copy or digital), simply add a section or annotate to show when your notes are related to social justice.

Periodically review your journal, looking for trends or patterns in your observations. Ask yourself how you can adjust negative trends to maximize equity, community, and agency through your teaching? How can you leverage positive elements further?

AM I SOCIAL JUSTICE ENOUGH?
RETHINKING "RADICAL"

Perhaps the biggest limitation to the successful growth of social and ecological* justice education movements is teachers' anxieties about their own legitimacy as social justice educators, particularly that they aren't radical enough to count themselves as social justice educators. If teachers are hesitant to identify social justice as a central part of who they are as teachers, it should not be surprising that social

---

* For me, ecological or environmental justice is included in social justice, as human animals are a part of the ecosystems in which they live. However, others make a reasonable point when they suggest that eco/environmental justice isn't given enough voice unless it is explicitly named. Throughout the book, when I reference social justice, it includes environmental issues. I use the term ecological justice when I am referring specifically to issues of ecological sustainability.

justice education is often considered an add-on or extra-curricular element of most schools. Later in the book, readers will be introduced to teachers who identify as social justice educators and their reflections on what it means to be a teacher with social justice commitments. For instance, Andrea shares the following:

> I have had conversations with people.... And they're like, 'Well, you're not wearing black... and trying to blow up banks, so how can you be an activist?' I think we have a very rigid view of what activism is, like it involves a placard and screaming.... And, to me that's not what it is at all. I think that for me, activism in my teaching is taking the opportunities to sort of poke at preconceived notions or assumptions that we may have.... The norm, as it were, what the norms of society are.

Other teachers with whom I spoke agreed with Andrea's statements. Dave, a retired high school principal, described his social justice perspective: "You could call me a maverick. You could simply call me someone who's committed to democracy and doesn't believe that we have to maintain the status quo.... I think we need to teach democracy in our classroom everyday. Teach and demonstrate democracy in our classroom everyday." Likewise, middle-school teacher Jennifer explained: "I think I certainly define myself as an activist.... A lot of people who I define as an activist... wouldn't see themselves as one, because they aren't chaining themselves to trees or going to protests. I don't think you need to do that.... Especially in education, it's about planting the seeds."

These teachers' words show us that the character of social justice education can be different than common connotations of social justice activists that circulate in the social imagination. Instead of protest and civil disobedience, their understandings of what it means to be a **radical teacher** center around ideas like democracy, unquestioned assumptions, and "planting seeds" that may allow students to take social justice in their own directions. This isn't to say classically radical approaches can never happen in the context of social justice education; however, these teachers focus their efforts on questioning otherwise unquestioned ideas and practices rather than in mounting directly adversarial protests. Some might suggest these "softer" approaches to social justice are too watered down to be effective. But, I suggest the teachers who I interviewed for this research are enacting social justice in ways that redefine radicalism, making it a concept more and more teachers can feel comfortable attaching to their identities. In the face of education systems that are historically influenced by traditions that place power securely in the hands of the teacher, these teachers have chosen alternative approaches. Their practices of teaching and learning emphasize education as a process of relating to oneself, others (near and far), and the planet, not an institution one attends to simply drink from a fountain of knowledge and become educated. These teachers doing education as a relational process despite the many challenges facing schools is nothing short of a radical act, one that pushes back on contemporary pressures for accountability and standardized testing that all but force teachers into rote coverage of densely packed curricula.

Teachers who feel insufficient to identify as social justice educators as a result of how many rallies, sit-ins, or letter writing campaigns they may or may not have participated in can rest assured these factors are not primary to supporting a social justice teacher identity. Social justice educators are defined by their commitment to enacting principles of social justice (like the ones discussed above) through their teaching. The remainder of this chapter offers suggestions for what this can look like within an educator's practice. These suggestions develop from and add depth to the social justice principles previously discussed.

SIX PRACTICE POINTS FOR SOCIAL JUSTICE EDUCATORS AND WHY THEY ARE IMPORTANT!

Every day educators make choices about how to bring their ideas for student learning into reality. Often those choices result in actions that allow learning to come into real life, while other times the choices are about how they think about the particular issues they are teaching, as well as the teaching processes by which the learning unfolds. Here, I offer a list of practices an educator could do to support identifying as a social justice educator. Of course, this isn't an exhaustive list, and it is not intended as a checklist against which an educator should be evaluated as "good enough" for social justice education. Rather, the suggestions are tools for helping teachers reflect on their professional identity in relation to forwarding social justice through education. I encourage readers to look for points of resonance and/or dissonance with their own teaching practice as they read through the following practices for enacting social justice education.

1) Give ultimate priority to developing inclusive learning environments.

A fundamental assumption of social justice education is that everyone gets to take part in a meaningful way (hooks, 1994; Monchinski, 2011; Sapon-Shevin, 2007; Wink, 2011). The most important thing educators can do to invite social justice values into their teaching is to develop teaching and learning environments that welcome all students to be active participants in the classroom community. While social justice education is most often understood as a political movement—and it is—this fundamentally social choice on the part of an educator recognizes that creating an inclusive classroom is a precursor for exploring social justice. Social justice educators pay deep attention to developing a learning environment in which a community of respectful learners can safely discuss political issues. In doing so, the introduction of social justice issues into classroom conversations often comes directly from students and not from the teacher. This is a sign that students know their ideas will be valued, even when others may not agree.

Laurie Frank's book, *Journey Toward the Caring Classroom, 2nd Edition* (2013), is an essential resource for classroom community building. It offers teachers a step-by-step guide to developing and maintaining caring classroom communities, which is a prerequisite for any meaningful engagement with social justice issues. Packed full of activities, the book offers concrete strategies for community building rooted in theories of experiential and adventure education.

Of course, any kind of broad statements about designing safe and inclusive environments can make the task sound easy, which it is not. The factors behind feeling excluded from a social environment are many, and to make things even more complex, individuals experience those factors differently. For instance, people who identify with a particular social factor like gender (man/woman/neither) or ability (able/disabled), experience what it means to be part of that category in different ways. This range of social experience makes it difficult to program a perfectly inclusive learning environment. For social justice teachers, then, the focus need not be on "getting it perfect" but on maintaining a reflective awareness of what is happening in the learning environment at any given time. Scanning the classroom on a consistent basis is one example of how to go about this reflection (see praxis point). It should be noted that people may feel excluded or otherwise out of place in a classroom despite the best efforts of their teacher and classmates. The complexity of social identities means there can be elements of inclusion that are outside the control of educators. Reflective practice strives not for perfection, but to push social justice educators to respond to the question: "Am I doing my best to teach in ways that make each learner a full member of the community?"

Praxis Point ✍ Scan your classroom a few times every day and ask yourself: Who is included in the learning community? Who may feel excluded? What can I do or say as the teacher to make the classroom as safe and welcoming as possible? Set specific scan times associated with classroom routines to make sure you are intentional about doing this. Notes from these scans can be recorded in your social justice journal (see praxis point on page 16).

2) Recognize and respond to the inherently political nature of education.

Whether an educator works in a traditional K-12 school environment or in an alternative setting; whether their classroom is of the traditional four-walls style or otherwise—all formalized education is political (Freire, 1970; Monchinski, 2011; Nieto & Bode, 2012; Wink, 2011). Sometimes the presence of politics in education is quite subtle or even invisible, while other times it is readily apparent to anyone choosing to watch or listen. Likewise, teachers respond differently to the presence of politics in education. Some teachers make these politics an overt part of what and how they teach, while others allow political aspects of education to exist quietly in the backchannels of the learning environment—noticed, but not always the central focus of teaching and learning. Some teachers ignore or deny that politics are at work in their classrooms; these teachers cannot be considered social justice educators. From my perspective, failure to recognize the presence of political ideology in the classroom (good, bad, or otherwise) ensures the continuation of the status quo in ways that do not reflect social justice values and may in fact perpetuate social injustice. This third group should not be blamed or scapegoated for the difficulties that exist in enacting social justice education. In many ways, these teachers are simply doing education as instructed by our education system.

Recognizing and celebrating that politics are a part of education is foundational to doing social justice work. When teachers and students are content with racism, sexism, poverty, environmental injustice, or other social justice issues, they make clear a political position. Naming and taking ownership for that position is a key part of being a social justice educator. Naming political viewpoints that pop up in educational environments (whether they arrive with teachers, students, parents, or are part of the institutional fabric of schools) counts as an action—it is a fundamental **doing** of social justice education. While simply naming the politics present may not seem like an action, I suggest it is a very active aspect of education because the ability to identify and react to the presence of political ideas gives teachers and students power to be active members of their communities. This power to name the cultural ideas that shape their lives—positively or negatively, is an example of the concept of agency discussed earlier as a principle of social justice.

3) Allow students' own voices to drive discussion and action around issues of social justice.

One major aspect of the political character of education is the authority vested in the role of the educator. This authority is not automatically negative; in fact, a teacher's exercise of authority based on experience and expertise is important for quality of learning (Dewey, 1918; 1937; Simpson, 2011). However, the teacher's authority also has the potential to constrain students' sense of their own legitimate knowledge. If the teacher is viewed as the absolute expert, the ideas and experiences students bring to the classroom may become devalued as students become accustomed to the teacher being the primary source of "right answers" within a learning community (Freire, 1970; Palmer, 2007). Social justice educators have an understanding that students are capable learners who bring their own ideas, perspectives, and experiences to any learning environment (Hewitt, 2001). They design learning experiences that intentionally foster students' confidence in their own ideas, their willingness to expose their ideas to criticism, and their ability to revise that thinking when useful new information is introduced to them.

Challenges to helping develop students' voices can arise in relation to issues of social justice. Students who identify as members of oppressed social groups may come into a learning environment in a deficit position in relation to their own sense of voice. This may be a result of a history of oppression or their individual, specific history. Likewise, students who experience relative privilege may lack awareness of their privileged position and how that position affects their fellow learners and teachers. Finally, it must be noted that the vast majority of teachers occupy positions of great social privilege, and that privilege cannot help but become bound up in the authority.

Social justice educators approach the facilitation of student voice with a high degree of tact, recognizing that every student is on his or her own voice-finding journey and developing an awareness of privilege and oppression. Students cannot be forced into having or using that voice to promote social justice. Planting seeds is a big part of helping students understand they are capable of thinking deeply and expressing their thinking clearly. These seeds may not grow immediately but can take root as students choose for themselves to assert their agency as citizens. Focusing on social justice education around the development of student voice and agency is a strategy for distinguishing social justice education from indoctrination.

Praxis Point ✍ Allocate specific times in the instructional day where pedagogy is driven through students' own words and ideas. This might take the form of community meetings, sharing circles, show & tell, or unconstrained journaling. Design opportunities for the community to offer feedback on individuals' thinking where appropriate.

4) **Be transparent about personal positions on social justice issues (Caveat: when/where appropriate and with great tact and respect).**

This statement offers contrary advice to what is stated in many social studies teaching resources. For instance, Kirman (2008) recommends teachers "be totally objective" and "avoid giving opinions on the issue" (p. 256). Meanwhile, other experts acknowledge the challenges and opportunities of teaching controversial issues, but leave an open question around teachers' personal stake in the issues discussed (Beal, Mason Bolick, & Martorella, 2009; Odhiambo, Nelson, & Chrisman, 2016). A social justice education stance assumes teachers hold political ideas about issues that arise in a classroom, and to withhold their perspective in the interest of neutrality is a denial of the political nature of education (discussed in practice two). Emphatically, this is not an endorsement of teachers "telling how it is" without restraint. Social justice educators must be intentional about when and how to inject their own views into the classroom community. The main thesis of this statement is that teachers should not pretend they do not have a perspective on issues of local and global community importance. A primary justification for educator disclosure on issues of social justice under study is that teachers have the opportunity to serve as examples of social justice supporters that students may not have in their family or community. Many teachers worry that injecting their own opinion into social justice discussions may unduly influence students' opinions, but some research suggests a teacher's ideology on a given issue is unlikely to sway students' opinions in coercive ways (Hess, 2009). While encouragement for educator disclosure of position on social issues is an important part of social justice education, this comes with several important caveats.

A key word in this suggestion for social justice education practice is **transparent**. Educator disclosure of opinion on social justice issues depends on a clear declaration that the teacher's position is simply an **opinion** like any other. While the educator may have strong feelings about that opinion, respect must be shown for individuals holding differing opinions. This level of respect requires teachers' opinions be introduced tactfully without ridicule or belittlement of those who think or feel differently, fostering the ongoing sense of safety in the learning environment. Chapter two further explores the idea of a learning environment suitable for social justice education being a place where students feel safe to disagree with one another, and also with the teacher.

Two final caveats remain about teacher disclosure: timing and legal contexts. Pedagogically, social justice educators should carefully time an introduction of their own political views into the classroom environment. In some cases, early disclosure may be an appropriate way to introduce a topic for discussion. In other situations, students may need some time to grapple with the complexities of an issue on their own before hearing what the teacher thinks (Hess, 2009). Effective social justice educators take stock of their classrooms to ensure the best timing for disclosure.

Praxis Point ✍ When planning to share a personal opinion in relation to an issue of social justice, carefully time your disclosure. It is unlikely your view will change a student's position simply because it is your position (Hess, 2009). However, consider whether having some time to work through an issue for themselves or in small groups may result in deeper thinking about the issue at hand than might occur if the teacher's position is shared at the outset.

Finally, social justice educators must also be aware of the legal context in which they are working. Some educational jurisdictions have legislated how teachers' political views can be introduced into a classroom (Hess, 2009). Social justice education movements oppose external constraints on how teachers are allowed to engage with their students (Kincheloe, 2008). However, direct defiance of these kinds of laws may not be a productive means of forwarding social justice concerns. Social justice educators working in areas where they are not allowed to share their ideas with students face a difficult challenge and are encouraged to implement other suggestions from this chapter in creative ways in order to best facilitate the development of social justice values in their teaching and learning environment. Meanwhile, concerned teachers, parents, community members, and even students are encouraged to take up democratic avenues for reforming laws that over-regulate teacher/student classroom dynamics.

5) Design learning experiences to promote curiosity and self-directedness in learners.

Part of a foundation for social justice education is harnessing students' curiosity into experiences that permit them to understand they are capable of finding out information and using it to shape their world both locally and globally. Working from an assumption that the purpose of education is to compel learners into further and deeper learning about a topic of study (Dewey, 1918; 1937), social justice educators seek to engage students as active participants in their own learning and not passive listeners dependent only on the teacher. Fostering such an inquiry stance (Watkins, 2012) requires tapping into students' curiosity and wonder about the world in which they live. Recognizing the importance of student voice, teaching approaches should adopt student-centered instructional methods, facilitating the development of voice through teaching strategies that engage learners holistically (e.g., hands-on, minds-on, hearts-on, spirits-on*). Such holistic engagement offers the possibility to activate students' innate human sense of wonder (Carson, 1965; Piersol, 2014; Sagan, 2001). If well facilitated, students' inquiries can be connected with classroom learning objectives. The intellectual engagement that is demonstrated through self-directed inquiry is a necessary precursor to the kinds of social action that are sought by social justice movements.

On the surface, this aspect of social justice education isn't especially political; the development of information agency in students can be equally applied to topics that are socially radical or totally uncontroversial. But, in another very important sense, fostering curiosity and self-directed learning skills is a major win for grassroots democracy (a big part of social justice campaigns), because it develops in young citizens the ability to be information actors rather than simply information receptacles (Freire, 1970). The politics of doing education in this way lies in the resistance to the mainstream of rote, teacher-centred instructional methods that flourish in contemporary schools. When schooling is dominated by high-stakes standardized tests and packed-to-the-

---

* This body, mind, heart, spirit conception of a whole person draws roughly on traditional Medicine Wheel teaching of the Anishnaabe First Nation people. For more explanation, see Bell (2014).

gills curricula, teachers often feel they have to resort to strategies for high volume information delivery in order to cover all the material. These strategies often squeeze out inquiry-based learning in favour of more time efficient methods.

6) Model a leadership presence demonstrating care and compassion that may inspire the same in students.

Popular understandings of social justice work convey images of aggression, radicalism, and violence (Bashir, Lockwood, Chasteen, Nadolny, & Noyes, 2013). The reality of social justice work is contrary to this conception. Leading social justice education advocates (Darder, 2002; Freire, 1970; Monchinski, 2011), including all of the teachers interviewed as part of my research, locate their motivation as social justice educators in feelings of care, compassion, and even love for their students— especially those students who experience social oppression. Of course, this doesn't mean teachers and learners for social justice never experience difficult emotions in relation to social justice. When contexts of privilege and oppression are examined, it is not difficult to understand why people seeking justice as a result of longstanding oppression would feel angry. However, anger is not the foundation of social justice or social justice education.

Naturally social justice educators would feel a range of negative emotions from frustration to rage as they watch students experience discrimination and marginalization, or perhaps even experience such oppressions themselves. Successful social justice educators will channel these feelings through a lens of care and compassion in order to design positive learning experiences for their students. Such channeling does not magically erase their negative emotions, but it may create opportunities for taking actions that generate hope for a more just future (Giroux, 2004).

Chapter Summary

❧ Social justice education is a confluence of equity, challenging privilege and oppression, building community, and fostering agency and action jointly enacted by teachers and learners in safe and inclusive learning environments.

❧ Teachers and learners are partners in the venture of social justice education. Social justice educators aim to share their power and privilege as educators by creating opportunities for students to guide their own learning, some or all of the time.

❧ Social justice education emphasizes positive relationships between all members of a learning community as a foundation for exploring the political issues that often divide communities and societies.

❧ Equity is a practice of ensuring all members of a community have the respect and resources they need to be full participants in the community.

❧ Challenging privilege and oppression means recognizing one's own experiences of privilege and oppression and then spending privilege to relieve oppression.

❧ Building community is a process of connecting individuals within and across aspects of privilege and oppression with the goal of building movements (Palmer, 2007) for social justice across many aspects of identity, culture, and community (e.g., racial justice, food justice, poverty eradication).

❧ Social justice educators foster agency and action in their students. Agency refers to "persons' ability to shape and control their own lives, freeing self from the oppression of power" (Kincheloe, 2008, p. 2). Actions are steps taken to fulfill and maintain one's agency.

❧ Possibilities for Practice
- Give ultimate priority in teaching to the development of inclusive learning environments.
- Recognize and respond to the inherently political nature of education.
- Allow students' own voices to drive classroom discussion and action around issues of social justice.
- Be transparent about personal positions on social justice issues.
- Design learning experiences that promote curiosity and self-directedness on the part of learners.
- Model a leadership presence that demonstrates care and compassion and may inspire the same in students.

CHAPTER 2 SOCIAL JUSTICE EDUCATION IN CLASSROOM PRACTICE
ENVIRONMENTS, IDEAS, & ACTIONS

Four underlying principles that inform social justice education are outlined in chapter one: Equity, challenging privilege and oppression, building community, and fostering agency and action. This chapter introduces three additional elements: Environments, ideas, and actions. These function as vehicles by which teachers can make the underlying principles discussed in chapter one become real. In other words, they are channels by which teachers can enact their interpretations of the underlying principles of social justice. Table 2.1 (page 29) shows how I define each of these terms. These definitions are offered as starting points for developing each element throughout the rest of the book.

The first part of this chapter looks at two main theorists whose work has contributed significantly to my thinking about social justice education: John Dewey and Paulo Freire. It is the work of these scholars (and others, too) that inspired my thinking about environments, ideas, and actions. Many volumes have been written about these two theorists individually, but a much smaller body of work examines the complementary aspects of their philosophies. These synergies are explained as I introduce the notions of environments, ideas, and actions as factors that enable the work of social justice teachers.

The focus of the second part of the chapter turns to hope and democracy, suggesting these two conditions both emerge from social justice education which comes to life through intentionally designed environments, ideas, and actions. Further, I explain that while the of environments, ideas, and actions helps to develop hopeful and democratic conditions, it is also sustained by tapping into hope and democracy as fuel. Maintaining this feedback loop contributes to the growth and energy of the movement of social justice education.

Table 2.1 Defining the Elements of Social Justice Education

Some exemplars are reproduced from Niblett (in press).

Element	Example
Environments include all of the *places and spaces* in which teachers and students interact. These include the physical environment (both natural and built), the social environment in terms of how people relate to one another, and the learning environment in which information is shared and developed.	The physical space of Tina's classroom is carefully designed to allow for students and teachers to interact collaboratively. She works hard to maintain a social atmosphere that complements this physical design. For instance, she stands at the door and greets each student individually as they arrive.
Ideas are the *concepts and stories* that in part constitute the interactions among teachers and learners. Ideas include, but can go beyond, the official curriculum. For instance, social justice topics not explicitly named in official curriculum can become a vehicle for required curriculum expectations.	Twelfth-grade students in a world issues class participate in a fasting campaign to develop understanding and awareness about local and global inequity to food access. In debriefing, they discuss how it felt to be hungry, how it impacted their ability to function, and the reality that their simulation is unlike the experience of chronic persistent hunger because of the ability to resume a privileged eating routine after a relatively short fast.
Actions are *doings*; behaviours that exist alongside ideas within the teaching and learning environment. Actions can bring ideas discussed in the learning environment to life, but, through reflection, can also shift and develop ideas held by teachers and learners alike.	Biweekly over two months, Kit's fourth-grade class works in collaboration with a local chapter of the Raging Grannies (http://raginggrannies.org/) to collect litter in parks near the school. Small groups work with a volunteer granny to sort and weigh recyclables, organics, and garbage, and to depict data in graphs and pictographs. Students discuss the value of parks as public spaces and the importance of taking care of natural areas to reduce impact. Together, they write up their discussions, digitize and post their graphs on the Raging Grannies' blog, and present recommendations to the parks department on placement of waste receptacles.

Praxis Point ✍ Social justice education is at its best when environments, ideas, and actions are intentionally designed and implemented by an educator in collaboration or conjunction with their learners. However, teachers' best intentions for implementing social justice education are challenged by the tendency for contemporary education organizations to function at high speed with high tension (e.g., packed curriculum, limited and/or fragmented time-frames, high stakes standardized assessments, competing priorities outside of school). There is no magic wand to be waved and solve this dilemma; teaching is hard! However, teachers who design regular reminders for themselves of their commitment to social justice education are more likely to deliver on these commitments even in the face of the overwhelming daily grind. An important part of this reminder is including a sense of kindness to one's self and forgiveness for the many ways in which our practices may fall short of ideal, especially for those who work in settings where social justice concerns are seen as peripheral to the main aims of education. Seek to name and celebrate the tiny, daily successes. These acknowledgements stand to promote the continuation of social justice education commitments over the long term.

Tip: Design one or more symbols of your commitment to social justice education. Place them where they can be seen often during your day (i.e., on the cover of your day planner/journal, above the classroom clock, in a corner of the black or white board). Let the symbols be a reminder of the kind of environments, ideas, and actions you want to drive your educational process. When appropriate, share the symbols with your students, making them a community reminder for how you want to live and learn together. Adjust the symbols as your community expectations for living and learning shift or change.

UNDERSTANDING SOCIAL JUSTICE EDUCATION: ENVIRONMENTS, IDEAS, & ACTIONS

John Dewey is often considered the preeminent North American philosopher of education of the 20th century (Apple & Teitelbaum, 2002). For Dewey (1897) and others who take up his ideas, learning environments are the fundamental feature of teaching, as they play host to "a process of living and not a preparation for future living" (p. 87) in focused and intentional ways that allow for thinking to arise, and thus for learning to occur (Dewey, 1933).

Likewise, Paulo Freire was an educator and activist in Brazil in the 1960s, where he developed a method of teaching literacy to poor farmers who weren't allowed to vote unless they could read. Freire's teaching was inherently activist, as his goal was to mobilize people by helping them understand their own oppression and take action against their subjugation in society. At the foundation of Friere's work is a notion called **Praxis**—a combination of thinking and action that has the potential to help people see themselves and their position in the world with greater clarity and address injustices that privilege some people and oppress others (Freire, 1970).

Dewey's and Freire's work have many synergies across the elements of environments, ideas, and actions. Some scholars (Monchinski, 2011) even suggest that Dewey's vision for democratic experiential education should be considered a harbinger of what would later become the critical pedagogy movement spurred by Freire. Likewise, it is of critical importance to understand that while Dewey and Freire are major thinkers whose works illustrate the centrality of environments, ideas, and actions over the past century, they are not the only thinkers whose ideas are foundational to activist education. Interested readers can trace citations throughout this chapter to other scholars and practitioners who continue to build on both Deweyan and Freireian philosophical traditions.

John Dewey and Environments for Social Justice Education

John Dewey's (1859-1952) work closely examines the nature of educational environments and the way these environments either facilitate or hinder positive learning (Apple & Teitelbaum, 2001; Simpson, 2011). I use the term environments to refer specifically to educational environments, including all of their physical, social, and emotional elements. Dewey (1918) argued that teachers never act directly upon students, but only on the environment that the students and teacher share:

> The only way in which adults consciously control the kind of education the immature get is by controlling the environment in which they act, and hence think and feel. We never educate directly, but indirectly by means of the environment (p. 18).

Working from this idea, environments become the most critical component of the conception of social justice education that I put forward throughout this book. By accepting Dewey's premise that an environment is the critical factor in the delivery of education, it follows that other elements of social justice education, such as ideas and actions, are dependent on the learning environment for their richness and depth. This does not mean that environment is of greater import than ideas or actions, but that environments hold a certain primacy because, as students and teachers come together, they must first meet within a particular learning environment before the teaching and learning of ideas and actions can begin. In a longer-term sense, there is a give-and-take relationship among environments, ideas, and actions because the social justice ideas and actions that unfold within a learning environment cannot help but contribute to the environment itself. However, some kind of environment typically exists prior to ideas and actions becoming an active part of the educative experience (Frank, 2013; Oakes & Lipton, 1999; Orr, 2002).

Deweyan Learning Environments

Social justice education can be cultivated by a particular kind of learning environment, and these environments are designed and maintained by teachers and students enacting particular ideas rooted in social justice and anti-oppressive pedagogies (Kumashiro, 2004; McLaren, 2009). Regrettably for the movement of social justice education, the predominant discourse in modern Western education has largely departed from the Deweyan thinking about learning environments described above. Whereas Dewey encouraged educators to think about designing learning environments as vehicles for delivering curricular outcomes, the focus in contemporary teacher education is one where environments are managed and controlled by teachers as a necessary precursor to content delivery, but not necessarily as an integral part of teaching and learning itself.* I want to be careful here not to establish a false divide between Dewey's concept of environment and a more managerial classroom management approach; effective educators need strategies for managing student behaviours and misbehaviours within the environments where their lessons unfold. Dewey (1918) himself used the word controlling to convey what he expected teachers should do with learning environments. But, there is a key difference in Dewey's understandings of what it means to control a learning environment and what is common in contemporary classroom management thinking. This key difference is **experience**.

For Dewey, experience is at the heart of education, and it is conveyed through environments. Dewey (1938) argues that all kinds of learning environments convey experience—that a human interacting in a particular environment necessarily collects experience in a brain-based sense because they cannot help but do otherwise. Our brains are constantly synthesizing sensations from our physical environment in order for us to have the kind of perceptions that make up what we call "experience" (Dewey, 1933). For Dewey (1938), though, while experience is the basis of education, not just any experience can be called educational—even and especially those that happen within the institution of schooling:

> The belief that all education comes about through experience does not mean that all experiences are genuinely or equally educative. Experience and education cannot be directly equated to each other. For some experiences are mis-educative.... It is a great mistake to suppose, even tacitly, that the traditional schoolroom was not a place in which pupils had experiences.... The experiences which were had, by pupils and teachers alike, were largely of a wrong kind. How many students, for example, were rendered callous to ideas, and how many lost the impetus to learn because of the way in which learning was experienced by them? (pp. 25-26).

An important takeaway from this passage is that, from Dewey's (1938) perspective, while there may be learning as a result of a particular schooling environment, it cannot be assumed that all learn-

---

* I suggest Levin, Nolan, Kerr, & Elliot's (2012) book, *Principles of Classroom Management* is exemplary of this approach, in which preventing misbehavior is apparently the primary goal of classroom environmental design.

ing is educational. For instance, a social justice educator who takes a group of students to a climate change protest may be mis-educating because early cognitive development, weak understanding of the issue at hand, or lack of preparedness for the events likely to transpire at a protest may result in students being unable to process the experience in educative ways. In this scenario, students may be alienated from the teacher's intended learning outcomes. This does not mean that students should never attend or design their own protests as a kind of social justice education, but suggests that careful planning is needed to ensure that specific social justice experiences are beneficial for the particular students who will participate. Dewey argues that educators are designers of learning environments and should make every effort to ensure their curriculum design, including planning, implementation, and subsequent reflection, serves over time to invite learners into other experiences that are richer and of greater depth (Dewey, 1938): "The central problem of an education based upon experience is to select the kind of present experiences that live fruitfully and creatively in subsequent experiences" (p. 28). For social justice educators, then, **just doing anything** for the sake of having experiences is not intentional teaching (Breunig, 2005; Jickling, 2009; Simpson, 2011; Smith, Knapp, Seaman, & Pace, 2011). There needs to be an understanding of how the **doing** connects to the specific outcomes that the **doing** is intended to achieve (Dewey). Specific and intentional design before, during, and after a learning experience is needed in order to facilitate the kind of meaningful involvement (Haras, Bunting, & Witt, 2006) that would qualify an experience as educative in the Deweyan sense. Haras (2003) defines meaningful involvement as voluntary participation in a purposeful and challenging activity from which personal satisfaction is derived. While the clause of voluntary participation is tricky in the context of school programs, which almost always have mandatory attendance and assessment requirements, the notion of meaningful involvement can still be useful in education to the degree that educators are capable of designing learning experiences that transcend required attendance and tap into students' potential to learn. In this way, social justice educators must design experiences that invite students' participation and are not coercive in nature. This is a critical feature of a social justice education learning environment.

Dewey's Theory in Action Today

Dewey's philosophical influence remains strong more than 100 years beyond the time in which he began writing. Larry Hickman (2012), director of the Center for Dewey Studies and a champion of the modern day significance of Dewey's philosophy, asserts that while his whole body of work remains important today, the critique of education is Dewey's most important legacy. In the face of standardized tests, teaching to the test, and back-to-basics mentalities that dominate contemporary discussions of education, Dewey's vision for quality education continues to offer plausible and practical alternatives. And yet, while Dewey's educational theories remain relevant, the practical implementation of those ideas in formal education settings remains more peripheral than mainstream (Apple, Gandin, & Hypolito, 2001). I offer two examples of innovative initiatives that I think exemplify Dewey's messages about educational environments and the kinds of experiences they can offer students. These examples are showcased with a view to the potential for mainstreaming the social justice elements of what are otherwise peripheral educational programs. Each example is further connected with the foundational principles of social justice education introduced in chapter one.

Table 2.2   Exemplar 1: "Reform Math" Instructional Approaches

(Special thanks to Nansi Harris for her research contributing to this exemplar.)

Exemplar	Channeling Dewey
Much contention surrounds the ways children learn mathematics in school. A shift away from rote use of rules and procedures toward encouraging students to experiment with their own algorithms has left many parents (and others) frustrated and confused. Searching social media platforms for "new math" or "common core math" reveals many snapshots of elementary worksheets and math tests asking students to show their mathematical thinking in ways that may seem strange and confusing. And yet, research has shown that with quality instruction, inquiry-based approaches to math education lead to greater understanding of math concepts and students who are less likely to make computational errors (Lawson, 2007).	Student-generated methods for solving math problems strongly align with Dewey's call for education to be inquiry-based. Simpson (2011) characterizes Dewey equally as "Mr. Science" and "Mr. Democracy." Likewise, math educators (Stocker, 2009; Stocker & Wagner, 2007) describe possibilities for teaching about social justice and democracy through mathematics. Teachers using student-generated approaches to develop mathematical understanding give students tools for problem solving, allowing them to develop deeper understandings of how numbers work and also the ability to pick apart difficult problems in order to understand possible solutions. Both these learning outcomes can be applied to Dewey's idea of a democratic society where ordinary people are given the skills needed for community decision-making.

• Social Justice Education Principles at Work •

Equity: Math is an equity issue! Success in mathematics at a young age is predictive of future success in a broad range of life domains including academics and employment (Stinson, 2004). Inquiry-based math approaches may begin to "level the playing fields" by helping students who struggle with traditional math-education approaches to gain access to knowledge connecting them with further education, better employment opportunities, and the skills to advocate for themselves and others using numbers.

Challenging Privilege and Oppression: Inquiry-based math approaches stand to challenge knowledge-privilege by working to close knowledge gaps that exist for socially marginalized groups, especially women and racial minorities (Flores, 2007).

Building Community: Reform math approaches often engage students in collaborative inquiry, where the challenges and successes of learning are shared in groups.

Fostering Agency and Action: Proponents of reform math education position math as a language and help students to develop number fluency by encouraging the practice of mathematical thinking, as opposed to rote repetition of facts, with a view to developing mathematical agency.

Table 2.3 Exemplar 2: Forest Schools

Exemplar	Channeling Dewey
Globally, a movement has emerged for school programing that extends beyond the four walls of a traditional classroom, and is, in fact, housed out-of-doors. Forest schools are typically pre-school and elementary schools that operate mostly or exclusively outside. Anne Stires (2016), a forest school teacher, characterizes forest school teaching and learning as "active learning, connected exploration, and dynamic play outside" (Loc. 202). Nature-based play experiences drive curricular learning goals, and many forest schools meet government approved curriculum expectations for the jurisdiction in which the school operates. For instance, The Environmental School in Maple Ridge, BC, Canada is a partnership between Public School District 42, Simon Fraser University, and other community partners. It operates as a public school delivering provincial curricula for any interested students (Blenkensop, 2012; 2014).	Rooted in learning through the natural world, forest schools show a strong link with Dewey's thinking about the nature of teaching and learning. Rona Richter and Lisa Molomot's (2013) documentary film *School's Out: Lessons from a Forest Kindergarten* (Trailer: https://vimeo.com/32463946) offers a scene where children are playing with a wooden ball, rolling it down a forest slope and using sticks and roots to experiment with how to change the ball's path. This kind of play-based learning, minimally structured by the teacher, is designed to engage students in inquiry. It epitomizes Dewey's assertions about environment-mediated learning through experimentation.

• Social Justice Education Principles at Work •

Equity: Environmentalism and participation in outdoor pursuits have become largely white, middle and upper-class phenomena (Ambreen & Berger, 2016; Gibson-Wood & Wakefield, 2013). Meanwhile, marginalized groups (by race, poverty, and other social factors) are more likely to bear the brunt of environmental degradation than privileged people (Norgaard, 2012). Forest schools aren't specifically designed to promote social equity; however, when public schools put environmental education at the centre of schooling, rather than in the margin, engagement with the environment can be normalized for all students. Accordingly, as these programs develop toward the mainstream, administrators of forest school programs should catalyze the social justice outcomes of their schools by developing access policies promoting and protecting some available spaces for students who may otherwise be excluded from forest school programming until such time forest schools are populous enough for any who wish to attend.

Challenging Privilege and Oppression: If as humans we are going to effectively address the ecological problems currently facing humanity (which are, in no small part human-generated problems), we must acknowledge that in deciding about how to dwell on the earth, we privilege ourselves to a much greater degree than our more-than-human (Abram, 1997) house mates (including animals, plants, and essential non-living elements like air and water). Forest schools' mission to recentre environmental education as both a curricular goal and vehicle for achieving that goal may be seen as a gesture toward spending our human privilege in ways that signal greater justice for more-than-human beings.

Building Community: "The teacher finds him/herself at the centre of a web whose threads are not only students but also place, parents, community, curricula, and life" (Blenkensop, 2014, p. 154). The act of doing schooling differently creates opportunities for new kinds of relationships among the members of a forest school community. The shift can change the dynamics of power so often held by the teachers and school authorities alone toward a model that is more community focused than institutionally bureaucratic.

Fostering Agency and Action: Environments, ideas, and actions unfold in an outdoor and ecological laboratory rife for exploration and experimentation. These processes are critical for the development and maintenance of curiosity as a foundation for inquiry (Blenkensop, 2012; Piersol, 2014) and self-efficacy as a foundation for applying one's efforts toward the making of a better world (Jennings, Parra-Medina, Hilfinger-Messias, & McLoughlin, 2006).

Paulo Freire: Ideas and Actions as Social Justice Education

Paulo Freire's work has had immeasurable impact on theories of education over the past half-century. He was an adult-educator and social activist who was exiled by the Brazilian government of the mid-1960s for leading a literacy campaign intended to empower impoverished rural people of Brazil (Apple, Gandin, & Hypolito, 2001). There are many underpinning concepts in Freire's work useful for helping contemporary social justice educators around the world to think about how and why they do their work. Specifically, Freire's focus on the importance of **love, hope, and freedom** as both conditions and goals for education resonate strongly for me, and I hope for many readers of this book. These compassionate concepts are a significant part of the elements of environments, ideas, and actions.

Freire's (1970) most well-known contribution to educational theory is a criticism of what he called **banking education**. In banking education, students are treated as containers into which deposits are made. The degree to which students are willing and able to passively receive the information being deposited and recall it on demand determines their success as learners. Freire challenges this approach to education because he argues that its fundamental purpose is to create passive people who are unlikely to challenge the status quo. In resistance of banking education, Freire suggests what he names problem-posing education.

Freire's Problem-Posing Education

Praxis, a keystone concept in Freire's problem-posing education can be understood as a bridging or linking of ideas and actions in order to solve meaningful problems. Mary Breunig (2005), who shares much of Freire's vision for education, asserts that praxis "starts with an abstract idea (theory) or experience, incorporates reflection upon that idea or experience, and then translates it into purposeful action. Praxis is reflective, active, creative, contextual, purposeful, and socially constructed" (p. 111). This way of thinking about praxis is useful for design of social justice education based in environments, ideas, actions. In calling upon reflection, action, creativity, purpose, context, and social construction, Breunig addresses all three of the vehicles for social justice education discussed in this book. Reflection and creativity are processes that bring ideas into being. Purpose links with the element of actions, placing the focus on doing in ways that bring about concrete changes in the world through social justice education. Finally, context and social construction concern environments in which both ideas and actions are incubated.

For the purpose of social justice education, praxis is a meaningful and practical connection between thinking and doing within a learning environment that helps students to see themselves as change makers for social justice in their own communities. To explain, let's return to the idea of discovery math explored earlier in relation to Dewey. Teacher and teaching theorist David Stocker (2009) tells us discovery math is useful because it gives students opportunities for making sense of math concepts instead of just memorizing facts. He points out, though, that the math may not really matter to students' lives: "Middle school is a wasteland of pizza party math, where youth are meant to... delight in figuring out the volume of the pizza box, how many slices each should get and how much it will all cost" (p. 11). For Stocker, the pizza party math content doesn't matter much to the broader context of students' lives. "Who cares?" Stocker reasonably asks. He suggests that, at least some of the time, math concepts can be taught through social justice content that will not only deliver learning about math concepts, but also a deeper understanding of the social dynamics that structure our worlds. Such a shift offers the possibility of bringing an element of praxis into teaching math, especially in cases where this new knowledge spurs students to take action toward creating a more socially just world.

Praxis functions as an educational gateway to Freire's (1970) more ultimate concept known as **concientizacion**, or critical consciousness raising. Freire (1985/2013) often described concientization as a way of "reading the world and… reading the word" (p. 411). That is to say learners use literacy skills to better understand the nature of the social world around them, including their role in it. They also learn how to identify when social dynamics create privilege and oppression that advantages some people and disadvantages others. This concept connects Freire's and Dewey's thinking about education. Contrary to popular perceptions of modern schooling, concientization assumes no separation between education and the real world—it is inherently a real world education. Freire says, "reading is more than a technical event for me, it takes my conscious body into action" (p. 150). These words demonstrate a clear connection between concientization and social justice education and indeed a link to Dewey's theories discussed earlier. Critical consciousness raising is not about developing knowledge in abstract ways, but about using knowledge in order to do and be in ways that make the world a more fair and inclusive place.

It is important to understand the sense of love and compassion that underlie concientization. Social justice activism is often perceived as being driven by anger and frustration, and while these feelings can be real and valid, it is a love for human potential that is the motivating force of social justice education and not hatred toward those who hold power in a society. Antonia Darder (2009), a champion of Freire's theories of education, describes her understanding of this activist love as:

> … a political and radicalized form of love that is never about absolute consensus, or unconditional acceptance, or unceasing words of sweetness, or endless streams of hugs and kisses. Instead, it is a love that I experienced as unconstructed, rooted in a committed willingness to struggle persistently with purpose in our life and to intimately connect that purpose with what he [Freire] called our "true vocation"—to be human (p. 567).

In other words, the ideas, actions, and environments that make up social justice education are rooted in a sense of educational purpose focused on helping people be better humans, with "better" being characterized by a commitment to inclusivity and justice for all people, and for the earth that supports human survival. This love is sometimes necessarily a struggle, as it is based in the realities that teachers and students face in an unequal world and requires the telling of difficult truths that acknowledge and name inequity.

Freireian Theory in Action Today

In Freirean models, social justice education is being and doing in ways that enact the sense of care and compassion teachers and students have for their shared humanity. Without necessarily acknowledging Freire's work, many contemporary programs share visions for education that prepare students to be change agents in their communities. The following example places a spotlight on these kinds of programs, particularly in the realm of alternative education.

Table 2.4 Exemplar 1: Oasis Skateboard Factory

Exemplar	Channeling Freire
The Oasis Skateboard Factory (OSF) is a publicly funded high school program of the Toronto District School Board in Ontario, Canada. The program serves students who are significantly disengaged from traditional schooling. OSF students earn high school credits in English, arts, and business as they design, manufacture, and market their own skateboards and skateboard culture products (Oasis Skateboard Factory, 2016). Founding teacher Craig Morrison explains, "It's not even a question of education anymore, it's a question of design. With the kids at Skateboard Factory, I want them to design their life and design their world" (Fielding & Barker, 2013, p. 12) He notes further that "Students who have never attended school regularly or got credits before buy into our mission ... they promote it, they're very serious about it" (p. 15). Morrison's words highlight the core praxis of the OSF program—meeting students in familiar cultural territory and offering them learning tasks that allow them to feel capable of acting in ways that make positive differences in their own lives and in the broader community.	OSF's focus on learning through real-world task completion and problem solving based in each student's connection to skate and design culture is exemplary of Freire's vision for education driven by reflection and action around themes that are meaningful to students' lives.

Table 2.4   Exemplar 1: Oasis Skateboard Factory (continued)

• Social Justice Education Principles at Work •

Equity: OSF serves students who are underserved by or alienated from traditional school programming. The program design begins with an affirming vision for creating positive and broader academics through connection and design (Fielding & Barker, 2013).

Challenging Privilege and Oppression: OSF students earn an honorarium for their participation in the program and may sell the design projects they produce. This financial incentive engages students who might not attend school because of a need to support themselves.

Building Community: The small classroom workspace makes for a learning community teachers and students describe as a family, with close connections to the local community both in terms of the physical community surrounding the school site and the regional skateboarding and design community (Fielding & Barker, 2013).

Fostering Agency and Action: Design as a framing concept for the program challenges students to see themselves as contributors to the world they inhabit, as opposed to onlookers whose world is designed for them.

© 2017, Blair Niblett, *Social Justice Education*, Wood N Barnes Publishing

BEYOND DEWEY AND FREIRE: PROMOTING DEMOCRACY AND HOPE

John Dewey and Paulo Freire have both made essential contributions to the concept of social justice education. I explore two overarching themes from their works needed for a deeper understanding of how social justice education is constructed: democracy and hope.

Democracy: Beyond the Ballot Box

Democracy is an ideological concept, and therefore, it is hotly contested. It is both a goal and an underlying principle of social justice education, but like all ideological concepts, it must be approached with critical caution. The idea of democracy can be challenging to take up within a social justice and anti-oppressive framework because the term has a wide range of meanings. It is frequently used flippantly or ambiguously and is often implemented in sociocultural systems in ways that do not reflect or achieve social justice or anti-oppressive goals, but instead reinforces the power of some individuals and groups and the marginalization of others (Carr, 2011b; Giroux, 2009; O'Sullivan, 2013; Schugurensky, 2013; Tupper, 2007).

Many schools function with a disconnection between an implicit commitment to democratic ideas and daily operations that hinder the flourishing of democracy. Examples of some practices enacted by schools that erode democratic ideals include streaming or tracking students into enduring ability groupings where students from low socioeconomic backgrounds are overrepresented in lower tracks (People for Education, 2015) and rigid curriculum structures that can limit young people's choices about what they want to learn. Defenders of the status quo in schooling might rebut these structures are necessary as young people do not know what is needed to prepare for a good life. However, the longer democratic engagement is delayed under the guise of protecting children (or even adults) from their own naivety, the more difficult it is for schools to claim they are interested in democracy as a way of living, beyond an occasional trip to the ballot box.

Teaching thicker democracy. Dewey (1918) offers a starting point for thinking about a thicker conception of democracy. By thicker, I mean that Dewey's understanding of democracy as "a mode of associated living, of conjoint communicated experience" (p. 87), centres more on guiding the development of community on an everyday basis than it does on the technical processes of voting to elect government or for the operation of that government (Carr, 2013).

Chomsky (2000) offers a somewhat clearer explanation of democracy, noting that, "in a democracy all individuals can participate in decisions that have to do with their lives" (Loc. 336). This way of understanding democracy clarifies Dewey's more abstract explanation. Dewey (1918) himself offers two characteristics by which the democratic ideal of a community can be measured: "the extent in which the interests of a group are shared by all its members, and the fullness and freedom with which it interacts with other groups" (p. 99). I do not interpret this criterion to mean a quest for absolute consensus but rather an interest that leans more in the direction of inclusion of diverse needs and interests than it does toward exclusion and marginalization (Abdi, 2013). Dewey's first criterion about shared interests is of particular importance for a democratic conception of education; a call toward equitable sharing of community interests requires thinking about power and privilege as elements of living together, and this has implications for the kind of teaching and learning needed to sustain democracy (Tupper, 2007).

Hoover (2013) describes a vision for richer societies and richer forms of education through animating the concept of democracy within schools. The notion of animation means giving tangibility to school-based learning so that students, in his words, "can think with, apply, and use the fundamental knowledge base of all subject-matter areas in real-world venues subsequent to their classroom and school experiences" (p. 125). One key means of making school learning meaningful is through the kinds of experiential approaches highlighted in case examples earlier in this chapter. Such programs and approaches engage students in relevant experiences, encourage intentional reflection on those experiences, and seek connections between such reflection and students' everyday lives. Through these kinds of experiences, students engage and practice the cooperative ethos of democracy first hand. Such ongoing practices of democracy can be a source of hope for the future as students learn, even in small ways, that equitable communities are possible.

Hope

Much like democracy, the notion of hope is a troublesome paradox because it can serve as a kind of mirage, leading to dashed hopes that are a demoralizing return on hard work invested by teachers and learners in environments, ideas, and actions for social justice. Indeed, the same forces that support the prevalence of thin democracy also benefit when social justice hopes dry up, and people succumb to the apathetic notion that things simply are the way they are (Freire, 1994; McLaren, 2009). On the other hand, hope is the ability to believe that just futures are possible. O'Sullivan (2013) notes, "if you cannot imagine a better future, it is impossible to work for it" (p. 175). What, then, is the use of hope in social justice education?

Is hope enough? The short answer to this rhetorical question is "no." Theories on hope in critical education strongly indicate that hope is necessary but is not sufficient in supporting social justice education. Specific conceptions of hope are needed. Kincheloe (2008), for instance, writes of "practical hope" (p. x), while Giroux (2004) uses the phrase "educated hope" (¶ 4), Freire (1994) describes "critical hope" (p. 8), and Fisher (2001) coins the term "cautionary hope" (p. 192). While each scholar here might offer slightly different emphases in explaining their conceptions, Weiler (2003) offers commentary that is broadly descriptive of the kinds of hope that sustain social justice: hope "does not assume a just and peaceful future is either inevitable or impossible, but asserts the importance of maintaining our values and goals and fighting for them in whatever setting we find ourselves" (p. 34). I describe this range of hopeful approaches as **anchored hope**, because the idea of hope is anchored to another related, and often more concrete, concept with the aim of preventing it from becoming merely a utopian prophesy.

Toward anchored hope. A common thread in anchored conceptions of hope is that the anchoring concept is transitive—that is to say it is a **doing** (like education) or, at least, it is connected to doing as a reflective component of praxis (as in critical, or cautionary hope). Freire (1994) asserts that, "hope… demands an anchoring in practice" (p. 9). For Freire, and for many other proponents of anchored hope, a praxis of hope comes into existence through struggles toward social justice. Activist and author bell hooks (2004) describes the importance of hope as a part of education for social justice:

> Hopefulness empowers us to continue our work for justice, even as the forces of injustice may gain greater power for a time.... My hope emerges from those places of struggle where I witness individuals positively transforming their lives and the world around them. Educating is always a vocation rooted in hopefulness (p. xiv).

Here, hooks alludes to struggle for positive transformation, both for the self and the wider world. Working from hooks' statement, I suggest that anchored hope drives the process of doing social justice, and works against the pie-in-the-sky mirage of false hope all too common in modern media-driven societies (Hedges, 2010). In demonstrating a will for change by doing something together, the efforts of teachers and students produce anchored hope as they work in tandem to concurrently learn about issues in their community and use that learning to struggle toward a more socially just world. Without hope anchored to praxis, activism lacks both purpose and direction—in the context of education, it then becomes aimless activity (Dewey, 1938) and could even be miseducative.

Chapter Summary

❧ Social justice education is enacted in teaching and learning settings through carefully designed environments, ideas, and actions.

❧ **Environments** are all of the places and spaces in which teachers and students interact. This includes the physical environment, the social environment, and the learning environment in which information is shared and developed.

❧ **Ideas** are the concepts and stories that shape interactions among teachers and learners, including required curricula and supplements used to complement the required curriculum.

❧ **Actions** are doings; behaviours that exist alongside ideas within the teaching and learning environment. Actions can bring ideas discussed in the learning environment to life, but, through reflection can also shift and develop ideas held by teachers and learners alike.

❧ Theories about educational environments for social justice are well developed through the work of John Dewey (and others working in a Deweyan tradition), who focuses on the importance of well designed experiences as the basis for education. Such experiences are primarily shaped through the environment in which they unfold.

❧ Paulo Freire and other critical pedagogy thinkers offer helpful theories of ideas and actions in social justice education. Freire's (1970) concepts of praxis (integrating thinking and doing into reflective practice) and concientization (developing a strong awareness of self in the world to become more fully human) work together to highlight the importance of educational experiences relevant to the politics of students' lives.

❧ In the broadest sense, social justice education is about promoting and practicing democracy and hope through teaching and learning. Democratic education practice means making every effort to include all students fully in the process of education. Hope means maintaining a belief in social justice principles (equity, challenging privilege and oppression, building community, and fostering agency and action), even in the face of short and long term setbacks or failures of social justice.

PART II 🔀 GETTING TO WORK

It is individuals who change societies,
give birth to ideas; who, standing out against
tides of opinion, change them.
Doris Lessing

ℒ *Meet the Teachers* ℒ

Throughout the next three chapters readers will encounter stories shared by teachers whose practice exemplifies social justice education across the elements of environments, ideas, and actions. These teachers represent a diverse cross-section of what it can look like to be a social justice educator.*

ⓒ *Andrea,* a high school teacher in her early 30s, has taught a variety of subjects (civics, history, family studies, and social science) for five years at several secondary schools in a rural city. In addition to classroom teaching, Andrea has supervised many extra-curricular programs including a peer counseling group and a gay-straight alliance. Since the time Andrea and I met for this project, she has moved from teaching high school to a university setting. Andrea shares "Being the Change" in chapter three and "This Has to be Deepened" in chapter five.

ⓒ *Mindy* teaches drama in a suburban high school and is within a few years of retirement. During our meeting, she conveyed an idea she shares with every new class she teaches: "People will forget what you say, people will forget what you did, people will never forget how you made them feel."** In apparent contrast with this warm relational notion, when I asked Mindy about her professional identity and social justice commitments, she described herself as "the old broad who won't shut up about what's wrong with the world." This offers some sense of the complexity of what it can mean to be a social justice educator—at once a relationship builder and a champion for fixing what's "wrong with the world." Mindy's story, "Blake and the Laramie Project," is in chapter four.

ⓒ *Dave* is a retired high school teacher and principal. Mindy references him as her principal in "The Blake and the Laramie Project." Dave has received several prestigious awards for his work as an educator, particularly for his school leadership strategies that harness students' inter-

---

* While the teachers and their stories are all real-life examples, their names have been replaced with pseudonyms (with the exception of Tim Grant).

** Maya Angelou quoted in *Worth Repeating: More Than 5,000 Classic and Contemporary Quotes* by Bob Kelly (2003, p. 263).

ests in pro-social change in order to positively (re)shape what he calls "the central narrative" of a school. Dave's story, "The Culture of Peace," in chapter three concerns the struggles and successes of developing a school culture centrally characterized by student-driven, teacher-facilitated human rights initiatives.

© *Colleen* worked four years at a private alternative school that delivered a five credit integrated program (outdoor activities, expeditions, community service learning, and some traditional classroom instruction) for senior high school students. Colleen also taught kindergarten in a private alternative school, taught in Ontario public schools, and taught at the post-secondary level. Colleen's perspectives on social justice education are slightly different than many of the other teachers who participated in this project. Instead of promoting an external "cause" or social justice objective, her focus is on making education, in and of itself, a means of realizing social justice. For Colleen, "The Act of Educating is an Act of Activism," which is the title of her story in chapter four. A second story, "Cross Country Curiosity," is found in chapter five.

© *Jennifer* has taught middle school in Southern Ontario for nine years. Andrea connected us; the two of them met during a teacher-training program. In addition to her work as a teacher, Jennifer is a musician and host of a popular podcast. Her social justice teaching crosscuts issues of sexuality, race, and social class. Jennifer tells her story "Planting Seeds" in chapter four.

© *Grace* taught for seven years at many urban high schools in contract positions before gaining a permanent job teaching geography. The heart of Grace's story shared here is love. Her sense of love as an educational imperative is directly evident when she tells about loving her job and her students, but also indirectly through ideas she shares about how she conducts herself and constructs her identity as a teacher. Grace's stories are "Students First! & Love!" in chapter three and "The Green Team" in chapter five.

© *Tim Grant* (who requested we use his real name) was a teacher for 13 years in the 1980s and early 90s. He left teaching to start *Green Teacher*, a magazine for teachers who are interested in environmental issues and integrating the environment into their teaching. Tim is a critic for the Ontario Green Party and ran for election as a Member of Provincial Parliament in Ontario in 2011 and 2014. Tim's temporal distance from the classroom and close connection to environmental education in terms of both discourse and practice, position him to offer commentary on the opportunities and challenges of the praxis of activist education. His story "Activist Trigonometry" appears in chapter five.

© *Zoe* is a high school teacher of more than 15 years. Currently, she teaches drama and English courses. I had the opportunity to visit her classroom as two teacher candidates I was supervising completed practicum under her mentorship. During one visit, students were reading Cory Doctorow's (2008) *Little Brother*, a novel chronicling the (mis)adventures of a small band of youth activists who challenge the tyrannical authority of the US Department of Homeland Security in a futuristic, dystopian San Francisco. Zoe talks about her choice to teach this novel in her story, "Subversive Literature," in chapter four.

© *Nate* has taught high school for several years. Currently, he teaches at an alternative school for at-risk youth that uses innovative programming in arts, media, pop-culture, and business to give students a positive experience after having been alienated from mainstream schools for a variety of reasons. Nate challenged me to justify why I was working in academia rather than directly with youth, and we discussed the best use of my time and talents in a world where so many youth struggle to reap the full benefit of mainstream education. This tone of playful scrappiness and passion for serving disenfranchised youth carried through in Nate's stories. Nate's tells "Brandon's Hand and other Stories," in chapter three.

These brief biographies are intended to entice readers to dive into the narratives that unfold in part two of the book. Readers looking for more depth on these social justice teachers may consult my doctoral dissertation through which the stories were recorded (Niblett, 2014), available online for free from the Lakehead University Library.

Reading Notes: The teachers' stories are printed in italicized text to represent the voice of the speaker as different from my voice as author. Every effort has been made to present the narratives in an uninterrupted way. However, at some key points where clarification is needed, or to prevent distortion of the speaker's meaning, explanatory text is offered. Remarks in [square brackets] represent an editorial comment containing contextual information needed to interpret what is being said, while {curly brackets} show an interjection by the interviewer, and are only used where it is required in order for the speaker's meaning to be understood.

Designing and Fostering Environments for Social Justice

This chapter expands on the concept of educational environments as a key element of social justice education. It begins with some ideas from invitational education, a contemporary movement of educational theory and practice founded in part on Dewey's (1918) democratic ideals discussed in chapter two. Introducing invitational education sets a context for the second part of the chapter where educators share their first hand stories of designing educational environments in their own teaching practices that support principles of social justice education. These stories offer inspiration and resonance for educators seeking to develop or renew their own commitment to social justice values. The chapter concludes with two praxis points offering examples or activities for teachers to try out in their classrooms.

Invitational Education

In summarizing the scholarship known as invitational education, Frank (2013) asserts that, "there is a ubiquitous mood in our education system that is uninviting" (p. 14). While she refers specifically to American public schooling, I argue that a similar mood pervades education systems in many jurisdictions. Social justice education offers possibilities for working against the often uninviting ethos of schooling, and, reciprocally, it is dependent on inviting environments for its successful functioning. Purkey and Novak's (1984) use of "inviting" transcends the common "welcoming" connotation attached to the word. Accordingly, these authors name invitational education as "the process by which people are cordially summoned to realize their relatively boundless potential" (p. 3). While this may feel like lofty language to describe welcoming conditions that support social justice outcomes, Purkey and Novak (2008) and others offer concrete principles for bringing their ideas to life in educational contexts. Readers will see similar applications in the stories of social justice educators shared later in this chapter. I offer the following meanings for each invitational principle in the context of social justice education:

- **Respect** positions people at the centre of education and presumes all people are valuable and should be treated as such. Respectful educators acknowledge that as valuable, capable, responsible members of a community, people who are affected by important decisions should have opportunities for some level of input on those decisions. In this way, respectful education demonstrates a democratic ethos by leaning toward **acting with** students, and not **acting on** them (Purkey & Novak, 2008).

- **Trust**, a process essential to making teacher/student interaction invitational, is characterized by attributes such as reliability, genuineness, truthfulness, good intent, competence, and knowledge (Arceneaux, 1994). The greater or lesser degree that these characteristics are present within an educational environment will impact the degree to which theories of invitational education become actionable.

- **Care**, like trust, reminds educators of the kinds of environments that are necessary to maximize educational ends. In invitational education, and in social justice education by extension, care is not an abstract concept but rather a conduit by which the teachers' and students' dispositions of "warmth, empathy, and positive regard" (Purkey & Novak, 2008, p. 16) are transformed into actions that further the aims of social justice in the communities in which the actors are situated.

- **Optimism** facilitates a realistic and hopeful approach to education, whereby all people are believed to have untapped potential of some kind. Educative environments must be designed to help identify and tap into that hidden richness.

- **Intentionality** gives invitational education a design mentality whereby every choice is made with invitational messaging in mind. As educators internalize an invitational ethical stance, it becomes more likely the unconscious choices and spur-of-the-moment decisions will reflect invitational principles (Stavros & Torres, 2006).

This is the **how** of invitational education. It allows for the other four assumptions to become actionable.

Operating from this intentional design framework, educators can work to increase the human potential of all participants to greater degrees than might otherwise be possible (Purkey & Novak, 2008). In one way or another, each of the principles of invitational education challenge long held ideas about how public education should operate. For instance, extending degrees of choice or input to students under the principle of respect can have many logistical barriers within the systems of schooling (the Goliath of standardized testing is a prime example). For those unable or unwilling to find ways that public education can change, even in small ways, it is easy to reject invitational education and other principles that underlie social justice education as simply unrealistic within public education systems. For educators, though, principles such as Purkey and Novak's (2008) are not all or nothing propositions (Niblett, 2008). Doing social justice education within conservative institutions may require small gestures that seem like tokenism, and may well be. However, these token changes, while only of small significance in the moment, may coalesce toward more noteworthy change through the continued efforts of teachers and students (Weston, 2008).

Crosscutting Purkey and Novak's (2008) invitational education principles is a focus on developing human potential. This is a strong point of resonance between invitational education theory and the broader mission of social justice education promoted through this book. The following are stories of teachers who are working to bring social justice principles, including those of invitational education, to life with their students.

In Their Own Words...

Dave: Culture of Peace

My second vice-principalship... I was sent there in February, so halfway through a school year. Now, Dunnvale High School, when I arrived there, had been understaffed in administration.... I went into a situation where there were fights almost every day, smell of drugs all over the school.... And, I really wanted to start building student capacity... because it's through students that we can change this.

And, it was a time when teachers were on work-to-rule—there were no sports. And, as a non-teacher now, out of the unions, I could offer things after school for kids, whereas teachers couldn't. So, I took some kids to a meeting... it was a police forum, a community forum.... Well, the police were being soundly attacked that night, by the press, and by others. And that wasn't the experience we had, and the kids were getting upset. We spoke up on behalf of the police. That began the advocacy. And, I asked the kids afterwards, do you want to get together once a month? We'll talk about how we can change things in our school, you guys can change things in our school, and we'll set a course. And, you'll get my support. That began the Culture of Peace.... So, that's how it started at Dunnvale... because we empowered kids.

It was one of those things that evolved from that initial meeting I told you about. There were two conferences being offered for kids, and one was being put on by the police, and I can't recall the name of it, and there was another one being put on, and it was called a Culture of Peace. And, it was held at police headquarters. So, I took these seven kids down just to see what it was like. And, it was run by a couple from Pottsville who were educators, and it was the international year for a Culture of Peace as designated by the United Nations. Well, it was such a hit with our kids, the speakers that they heard, that this international conference at the UN came up, and... we found them money to take them down there. From there, the discussion started. What are issues at our school? And, I still remember coming back on the bus from New York, these kids had done phenomenal things. Like, it was long days at the UN with kids from all over the world. And, at the end, the kids had to come up with a mandate and declaration that they would present to the United Nations. I found out after it had been presented that the process had been waylaid by UN staffers, and that it wasn't what the working group had wanted to present. Our kids gathered up everyone at the hotel that had been there, and they pulled an all-nighter and re-wrote it and presented it at the United Nations the next day, and said, basically, "You guys screwed up, you tried to railroad us." And, I was so damn proud of them because they had taken that stand. And that stand was so important, because they knew they had gotten the support, they had gotten the backing, and that is what started the Culture of Peace for our school. Then, it was student driven.

So, they developed a whole variety of projects.... The very first one that these kids put together was a white bandana anti-violence campaign at Dunnvale High School, because of the gang violence. The kid that brought it forward, his cousin had been murdered by gangs. You know, we made bandanas, which you're not allowed to wear in schools. Our home economics class actually dipped them in UN Blue, and kids could wear them around their arm, or their sleeve. And, they came out with posters, and the kids in media-tech developed the posters, and we had speakers, and announcements every day. So, you know, there's many layers, and each campaign became multi-layered, so it would go on for two-weeks, and these bandanas were only given out in the last couple of days, and it was... big, it caused discussion, and what you want to do is cause discussion. Let kids talk about it.

A similar thing happened at Riverside Collegiate, a group of the drama kids said, "You know, there's a lot said about victims, uh, what about the silent victims?" So, rather than a moment of silence, a moment of noise.... And this happened during the White Ribbon Campaign [against men's violence against women]. So at lunch time—and you know, we discussed this well in advance, and I primed staff on it, and we put a couple of extra staff in the cafeteria—the kids from Drama started at the end of the hall with drums, bugles, noise-makers, placards... down the hall the entire length, right into the cafeteria. Bang, bang, bang, noise, noise, noise. And then all of a sudden—Stop! And as they stopped, different females stood up on top of the tables with tape across their mouths and slings on their arms, with some sort of damage to themselves, and nothing was said. And, they stepped down and they walked out. That caused discussion; that is what you want. They went in, distributed information around, so there was something there to support it, and teachers were ready to discuss it afterwards. That's what Culture of Peace is about. It's advocacy, it's giving kids the power to do things that are important for them, to bring about change.

Empowering kids to create and generate ideas, and activism, if you will, around issues that were important to them. Because, remember, a lot of these kids were minority groups, or were made to feel different, or were different. [It] gave them a safe place to be, and a safe place for advocacy, and a place to open discussion. And... talk about impacting literacy and numeracy.... Attendance went way up, because kids wanted to be there.... You know, a school that was typically middle of the pack for literacy and numeracy scores, in those six years that we had this going, we stood first in the board on two occasions, and we never dropped out of the top five. And, yeah, we still focus on literacy and numeracy, but what we did was we addressed it through student advocacy.

ⓒ Andrea: Being the Change

I think that in teaching, you have the opportunity to have mean-ingful conversations, and I think that for me, activism in my teaching is taking the opportunities to sort of poke at preconceived notions and assumptions that we may have about gender, or race, or class, or, you know... what the norms of society are. And, the classroom is the perfect place to start those conversations.... And, it comes out in lessons, but it comes out organically... Like, it emerges in conversation.... You listen to the students.... kids will be talking about an issue in a school, let's say, the football team.... about the resources that the football team gets versus the junior girls' basketball team. And, why is that fair? Well, it's not fair. Right? And so, just because it's not part of the lesson plan and part of the curriculum per se, it's still a very important conversation to have. Why does it make people angry? Why are some people defensive? Why are some people on the offensive? You know, why do we put so much stock in football, which is a predominantly, almost exclusively male enterprise in schools? But, the curriculum documents open up the door for critical conversations, you can grab hold of those strands... have those conversa-tions in your classroom, and nobody can come to you and say that it isn't based in the curriculum.

I think that for me.... when I started teaching, it was like... I'm an ac-tivist and I can make my students activists too, right? And I can sort of... share my views with them, and they're obviously going to see that those views are the right ones [sarcasm]... and then I'll like have this army of teens who go out into the world and think like me. And, then the world will be a better place. But, that's really problematic. You can't do that. You can't do that to somebody. And so, that's why I'm now at the point where I see it [social justice education] as the start of a conversation.

Kids are smart. And... their whole life... as teenagers is being im-posed upon by adults. And... kids called me on it... in their own way.... That I was imposing my values on them. And, it doesn't come out that way... they don't say "You're imposing your values on me." They say like... "Screw you, I don't want to do this!" Or you know, they tease you... or... there's power struggles, right? And, those were important power struggles for me to... define my own position, but also to understand that... I'm an educator... that I can provide a certain environment, and I can be very clear about what my standards are in that environment, and what my values are... like transparency is really important. But you're never

*going to have an authentic conversation unless other voices are allowed
to be heard.*

*I had many difficult, frustrating, upsetting conversations with kids
because I opened up this Pandora's box when it came to social justice issues like race or gender or whatever, and, when I think back on it, it was
very upsetting for me at the time to hear people say racist or sexist things.
But then I realized that it was a testament to the environment that I created that those dissenting voices could be heard....*

*I think this is where... I see an evolution in my thinking, right? Like, I
think I was very "be the change" when I started. And... I still think that's
a very powerful notion... I actually had that printed on a piece of paper
and put it on the front of my desk for my very first classes ever. But, I think
that what that looked like, what being the change looked like to me when
I started teaching was very different from what it is now.... I was very
gung-ho and felt like I can really create all kinds of change, and influence
kids, you know? And, the kids needed saving, and I was going to be the
one to save them.... But, again.... I couldn't expect... that they would
start the semester with me, being one way, and then by the end they were
like, you know, activists.... So, one of the key theories that influenced me
was anti-oppressive education.... Kevin Kumashiro and Ellsworth,* and
all the rest.... Because... it's a way of looking at the classroom as a holistic
experience... and looking at the way you deliver the curriculum, the way
you act.... It's kind of like a self-reflective assault on everything going on
in a classroom... In a good way.... I think that is the only way that I could
do activist education, as I became more comfortable... and could see the
potential power that I had to influence students.... So, anti-oppressive is
really important to me because it is rigorous self-reflection about all of
the power dynamics in the classroom. Which includes the power invested
in the role of the teacher.*

Nate: Brandon's Hand, and Other Stories

*One of my favorite stories is, I guess last year, I had a big boy, 6′4″
kid, gangster, drug dealer, tough, massive, I absolutely loved him. Loved
the kid. And, there was an issue where, again, it extends from their family and stuff. So, he was angry with something happening at home, and
I was you know, in his face at the time trying to help him, and he got
angry and he left. And you know the old school doors, where there's the*

---

* Kumashiro (2000) and Ellsworth (1988)

glass, and—[Int: With the wire mesh inside? Ya!] he punched that. And it went straight through. Beautiful circle. So, he punched the window. And, he was walking out of the school, and I followed him, and I'm like, "Brandon, «commheer»."

And, he comes back. Like, anyone else would have been scared that he's going to, you know, beat them. He's huge. And he comes and he's like, "Um, sorry, sir." I'm like, "It's ok, show me your hand. Ok, come with me." So, I took him to the sink and washed his hand, and he was apologizing. I'm like, "Alright, mate." And then I bandaged it up, and I said, "You have to go to the medical centre, you might need stitches. You wanna go?" Because he was over 18 at the time. He's like "Ya, I'll go." Then I said, "By the way, that was a fuckin' good punch. I'm glad it wasn't my face. You would have done some major damage." And he just smiled and left.... To me, it's the kids, and part of the social activism is that you care. And they know Nate's there—not to bust their balls. Sometimes I will, and I've got nicknames at school, but it's because I care.... So, it doesn't matter if I'm black or white or gay, or whatever, it's this is a human being who takes interest, who really gives a shit, and maybe we can learn something from him.

I had a kid a couple of weeks ago… and he's not very bright. I love the kid to death, but, he's an idiot. So, he got angry a couple of weeks ago, and told me to fuck off. Whatever… we dealt with it. He was suspended, there was other stuff. It wasn't about that he was suspended. He came back in the other day, and he wasn't supposed to come in, he's been shipped out. And, like, he walked in, he's "Hi" and I'm like, "You going to tell me to fuck off again?" And he's like "Hi," and I'm like, "Sit down. We'll talk." You try to help him out. So, this kid has been suspended 25 times, he's on serious charges, he's a drug dealer, he's a gangbanger, he's an idiot. Like, if the best thing that happens to him is that he knows there was a couple of people at [this school] that really cared for him, maybe that's going to resonate in the future. Maybe when he has kids. That's activism, I think. It's simply, it's not about burning a building or driving a car into something to get attention, that's not what it is for me. I'll work more in the background.... I think that if a community feels valued, then a community can contribute to society, and members of the community can be great human beings and great citizens.

ⓖ Grace: Students First! & Love!

Students first! Although I came into this [teaching] with a passion to share, an inspiration to do good in the world… for me, it's all about do-

ing my best for the students, and making sure that they leave feeling like they can do, and they are successful. So, I guess the first thing that drives me is the real belief that all students can be successful and all students can learn. And it's about the type of environment that we enable that will allow students, or hold them back. I think there are so many barriers in a school that can hold students back, rather than help them to be successful. So, every year that goes by I'm finding myself a little more successful at helping them. That's where I see my biggest goal. So, before it is about... changing their views of the world... it's about making sure they have the skills to do what they want, you know, to be successful in their way. So, in that way, maybe activism has taken a back seat, my own beliefs about things so that there's, they have more power to be activists in their own way, right? That's a natural progression for a teacher to want to do that.... Because in the first few years, you're just trying to learn the curriculum, and cover the things, and do a good job.... Now, you're like, okay, so this person is struggling with this. Why? How do we change that? So, that's number one for me.

People are really nervous about the word "love" in schools. So, I think that's probably the way I'm an activist. I use that word really comfortably, and, um, passionately. I love my students. I love my job, and I love the earth.... And, I think that makes for an important element of my teaching, because when you love something, and you explain that to kids also, like, when you love something, it's unconditional. And, what more beautiful thing is there than that? Because, you can work through anything and it makes you feel good, and you know... you don't give up on things when you love them. And I say it, you know, "I love you guys," "I love this!".... Ya, I use that word a lot, and... I think that's probably important too because it keeps you remembering what's important.

And, like, the first time you say it, they'll all be like "whewwwww!" and... I might be frustrated one day about the way things are going, and people might not be doing their homework, and maybe there's been some racist comment in class.... And, using that word might get everyone off guard the first time, so you have to explain yourself. But, then all of a sudden you've gotten a little closer with your class by... acknowledging that, yes, I do love you, and love this job, and it makes it hard when you act like, you know, none of this matters. 'Cuz it matters a whole lot. To you guys, you know for your goals, and to me to feel like, you know, we're here doing something special and important.

Praxis Points
Learning Activities for Developing Social Justice Education Environments

Literally hundreds of books exist to help teachers conduct activities intended to bring about positive learning environments (Frank, 2013; Stanchfield, 2014). Many of these aren't explicitly about social justice education, though some lean in this direction (Keegan, 2012). The following are activities to help social justice educators get started or veteran teachers shake up their routine for setting a learning context that is aligned with principles of social justice education. In each case, I offer a framing or reflection focusing explicitly on issues of social justice. If a teacher wants to present one of these activities without an explicit social justice focus, each has intrinsic features that would help to develop an inclusive environment conducive to social justice education.

Activity🏀 Energy Ball

From *Teamwork and Teamplay* (Cain & Jolliff, 1998)

How to Play

Form a circle with your group. Create an imaginary ball of energy between your hands (a sound effect marking the balls appearance can help). Encourage group members to practice creating and shaping their own energy ball. Once the concept of the energy ball is understood, teach the following moves for passing the ball:

- Level 1
  - › **Pass:** The energy ball is passed either left or right around the circle using a cupped hand passing motion.
  - › **Reverse:** Change the direction of the ball by a vertically positioned forehand that blocks the pass of the energy ball and forces it in the opposite direction.
- Level 2
  - › **Bounce:** Maintain the direction of the pass, but skip a player by bouncing the ball at his/her feet. The further adjacent player takes control of the ball and plays it onward.
  - › **Over:** A two handed forward tossing motion that sends the energy ball to a player across the circle. The receiving player is obliged to make a left or right pass.
  - › **Pop:** Disintegrate the energy ball with a puncturing motion and recreate a new ball. Is it big? Tiny? A heavyweight?

Featherlight? How does changing the nature of the ball necessitate changes to the movements of play? Only your group will know.

- Level 3
  - › **Schwa:** A high risk maneuver for experienced players! Reverse direction and skip a player by signaling "Schhhhwaaaaa" while passing the ball in an around-the-back passing motion. Adding a spin for flare is also encouraged.
  - › Other moves as inspired by the energy of your ball.

Continue playing as long as the group's energy ball emits positive vibes. If you're interested in digging into the metaphor of group energy, check out the following reflection ideas. If not, the activity is still likely to generate positive vibes for your group.

Questions for Reflection
- In this game, we've been playing with energy by creating and recreating an energy ball. What did the energy of our group feel like as we were playing and learning together?
- How can we consciously create the energy of our group so that everyone has maximum inclusion and participation?

Activity⚖ Concentric Circles of Social Justice

In this variation on a classic get-to-know-you activity, participants will interact through an organized rotation to complete partner tasks and talk through issues related to social justice. Thanks to Jennifer Stanchfield (*Inspired Educator, Inspired Learner*, 2016) and Adventureworks! Associates for these ideas.

Set-Up & Play

Organize your group into two concentric circles (one inside the other), with partners facing each other (outer circle facing inward, inner circle facing outward). Tell participants they are going to be assigned a series of small tasks to complete or topics to discuss with their partner. After each round, one circle will rotate and participants will be aligned with new partners.

The concentric circle formation provides an opportunity for focused and structured interaction between partners. The specific nature of each interaction is up to the facilitator, based on identified group needs. I suggest interspersing social-emotional learning and community building partner tasks (serious play!) with short tasks or conversation prompts related to specific social justice issues relevant to the group's context or learning outcomes. This format allows for breaking up heavy discussion with rapport-building tasks that allow for the demonstration of trustworthy behavior between partners. Consider the following activity and conversation ideas.

Add'em Up	On "go," partners throw up a hand from behind their backs showing between 0 to 5 fingers (each partner uses one hand). The goal is for one partner to add up the total number of fingers and yell out the correct answer before the other partner. After success adding to ten, add to twenty using 0 to 10 fingers (each partner uses two hands).
Finger Jousting	Partners shake hands by wrapping their hand around their partner's wrist and thumb with index fingers pointed at the partner. Points are scored by touching the shoulder or quad of your partner, while keeping your feet planted on the ground. After playing with right hands connected, switch grips and play with left hands connected.
The Bends	Partners shake hands with their right hand and pick up their own left foot with their left hand. The goal is to unbalance the partner so that they release their foot to regain balance. Meanwhile, maintain balance yourself as your partner tries to make you release your foot. After playing with right hands connected, switch grips and play with left hands connected.
Toe Jam	Partners place their hands on each others' shoulders. The goal is to use their feet to tag either of their partner's feet while trying to avoid being tagged.
Aura	Partners begin this activity standing palm-to-palm. They then close their eyes, break palm contact, and individually spin 3 times. The goal is to resume their initial palm-to-palm contact without speaking or opening their eyes.
Talk About	One partner talks on a topic (i.e., last movie you saw, best meal ever, dream holiday) while the other partner listens. The speaker must continue to speak and the listener may not ask questions or respond in any way. The facilitator lets partners know when to switch roles.

Partner Tasks

The following social justice tasks and conversation prompts are intended to highlight a breadth of social justice issues. You might use them as a way of introducing the concept of social justice in its various forms. These topics are obviously more contentious than many of the community-building partner tasks. This may not be the right choice for every group. As a facilitator, make sure you **know your group** and assess their readiness for these kinds of conversations. I am a strong believer in the need for making room for difficult conversations, even if they may feel uncomfortable. Still, **timing is key**. Participants may be won over to the importance of social justice if they are introduced to these ideas in careful ways by a caring facilitator. Consider developing your own prompts to fit the local social justice context in which you are working or just do the community-building, partner activities if your participants need more time to prepare for unpacking privilege and oppression. In many ways, community building is the first step toward starting conversations about social justice.

Social Justice Tasks and Conversation Prompts

- Talk about the positive aspects of living in a diverse community.
- Talk about ways you experience one or more kinds of social privilege. How does this privilege help you live well?
- What does racism look like in your community? How does it impact all of the people who live in the community?
- Talk about ways that girls and women are awesome! How might girls and women experience disadvantage as compared to boys and men?
- Hold hands or slow dance with your partner for 30 seconds, no matter your gender/sex or their gender/sex. Is this awkward? Why or why not? What aspects of privilege or oppression might be at play here?
- What does poverty look/sound/feel like in your community?
- What advantages do people in the global-north have that people in the global-south do not have?
- Look around the room and assess whether the space you are in is accessible to someone using a wheelchair or other mobility device. How might it be difficult to navigate the world with a mobility disability?

- Talk about your cultural identity (and/or what counts as a cultural identity!)

Questions for Reflection
- As an inclusive learning community, what were our best attributes during this activity? What are some attributes we might want to work on or change?
- What assumptions were made as we went about interacting with our partners? What are assumptions and how do they arise?
- What makes it difficult to talk about social justice issues? How can we work toward talking more openly about issues of privilege and oppression?
- How can we act as a learning community to increase justice around the range of issues we've discussed in this activity?

TAKING ON IDEAS FOR
SOCIAL JUSTICE EDUCATION

With the development of environments established as the foundation for social justice education, ideas and actions can interact as facilitating factors in learning. The interplay of ideas and action (the concept of praxis described in chapter two) come alive in the Praxis Point moments shared throughout the book. As pertains to social justice education, the element of ideas has two broad facets. First, it is about specific experiences of social justice and injustice related to the issues and examples that present themselves for various individuals and groups (for instance, "isms" like sexism, classism, ableism, consumerism, environmentalism). At the same time, it is about developing and redeveloping understandings about social justice itself.

Isms are pervasive in social justice talk; for instance, sexism and racism are usually assigned negative connotations, while feminism and environmentalism are generally considered positive within social justice circles. Isms and ism-talk are useful for social justice insofar as they serve as thinking tools for helping people understand their values and put those values into practice in their daily lives. At the same time, an ism can be challenging if it becomes a hindrance to turning social justice values into lived practice. In my experience, this hindering tendency can come about in two main ways. Sometimes, an ism can become so ideologically loaded that it has difficulty drawing people together to form movements that can effectively act on the issue. In this point of caution, I am not dismissing progressive or even radical politics (indeed, the world needs radical ideas!), but suggesting that social justice activists are most effective when their most radical ideas can exist in parallel with broader progressive ways of thinking so that movement-developing dialogue can unfold (Palmer, 2007). A second hindering factor of social justice isms can be seen if ideas become too abstract and would-be movement joiners fail to see the relevance of the ideas to their own lives. Again, my caution here is not absolute, as abstract thinking can be important for the development of an idea. However, if the only kind of thinking available to a social justice movement is abstract theory, it may be difficult to gain traction by engaging in praxis. One possibility for maximizing the effectiveness of isms as social justice ideas is to anchor them securely in broader principles of social justice, like those introduced at the outset of chapter one.

Principles of Social Justice Education:

- Equity

- Challenging Privilege and Oppression

- Building Community

- Fostering Agency and Action

The four principles of social justice education suggested in chapter one can serve as starting points for what it means to do social justice; however, they must be the subject of regular ongoing reflection and perhaps revision as new understandings based on experience and reflection arise. Remember that conceptions of social justice are not static; rather, they shift and change dynamically as teachers and students engage in the praxis of social justice education. This development of our understandings of social justice is not, for the most part, accomplished through formal proceedings, but rather through everyday reflection on the experiences we have in living our social justice ethics. Jickling, et al. (2006) describe this process of idea regeneration as a way of **doing** ethics:

> Ethics is an open-ended process with the potential to expose new challenges and generate new possibilities. It is a process of making choices that enable better ways of seeing and doing things. This doesn't mean that decisions and actions are never taken—we do act. It does mean, however, that ethical positions are open for discussion, re-examination, and revision (p. 2).

Such open-ended and recursive weaving of action and reflection makes for a powerful practice of ethics as social justice education. The teachers' stories shared through this chapter show this weaving at work. The ideas cited in their stories are diverse, ranging from LGBTQ activism to radical literature study to big questions about the nature of inquiry as a social justice idea. While not taken up explicitly, they also touch on the key principles of social justice which are the foundation of this book: equity, challenging privilege and oppression, building community, and fostering agency and action.

IN THEIR OWN WORDS...

Zoe: Subversive Literature

So, with Little Brother *[Doctorow, 2008]... a friend of mine... said "You need to read this..." And... I fell in love with the subversive nature of it, the activist nature of it. The fact that students could be activists was really meaningful to me... I just kind of lucked into it. And then, I contacted Doctorow and told him I was teaching it, and so, ya, so he tweeted with me, and I was able to show my students that, and then I sent him a bunch of the resources I created and he's uploaded them onto his site*.... So, he was writing my students. So that makes it a gift on its own.*

I think, if I'm not subversive in my teaching, then I am not teaching. [Interviewer: Could you say more about what you mean about subversive?] *I mean pissing somebody off. I also mean challenging what the expectation of normal is. I also mean... re/presenting—and not «representing»—but, re/presenting the notion of knowledge. I always want my students to explore their own assumptions. And, maybe this is my cultural studies background, but... if they aren't second guessing and triple guessing themselves—and by subversion I mean subverting even their own thought processes... then I don't think, I don't want them to regurgitate facts. I want them to become critical thinkers, so that they can change things around them.*

And part of that comes from my heart, that if I don't feel it, I'm doing something that isn't making a student go, "Wow, hey, woo!" then that is not inspiring learning. And... I also believe that I can be subversive teaching Macbeth. *So, sometimes it's about what I teach. Often it's about how it's taught, but certainly with* Little Brother *and... with most of the texts... I like new texts, because if I'm inspired by it then I want them to be inspired by it as well.*

Jennifer: Planting Seeds (Or, How Not to Be a Jerk!)

We recently did... an identity day, and you had to sort of identify three elements of your identity, and one of the ones that I chose was activist. I mean, I decorated my door of activism. So, I think I certainly define myself as an activist, and I think I'm always sort of finding new things to

---

*http://craphound.com/littlebrother/2012/06/03/remixable-grade-10-course-materials-for-little-brother-2/

be an activist about.... I would say that sort of, my main focus has been and continues to be LGBTQ stuff... but I'm sort of you know, working on like classist things, and Aboriginal issues, and they're all intertwined, ultimately. But... ya, I think it defines me. I guess I could see how there are probably a lot of people who I would define as activists who wouldn't see themselves as one, because they aren't chaining themselves to trees or going to protests. But, I don't think you need to do that. Especially in education, right... It's just about planting the seeds.

This is the time of the year that I really start to notice that it's working. I have a student teacher right now who's... doing drama. And, she was doing an activity with my students about... this kid that was getting bullied. And so, she asked the kids to come up with reasons why the kids were bullying him. And, ah, one kid puts her hand up, and she was like "Because of his class?".... I could see the student teacher stop and think, "Why would they bully him because of what class he's in?" And, then she realized what the kid meant, and she was like, "Oh! You mean social class!" And I'm sitting there like "YES!".... It's neat, it's neat. Because, they get it. Grade 8 especially, they're kind of hungry to form their own opinions about things.

I think that curriculum content is important, but it's meaningless without... that character education piece, without that critical thinking piece.... Cuz really, what kid remembers when confederation is? You know, as long as they know how to... find a source that they think is reliable, to find it out. That ability to learn and to find knowledge is more valuable than any facts. And, how to not be a jerk.... I think that's fundamental. I guess when it comes to like a teachable moment or something, I'm not the teacher that's like, "But we have to learn this thing about biology!" You know, if a kid has a question or there's something going on, you know.... Those are the moments that people remember from school anyways, like when you have a real conversation about something other than, I don't know... Pythagorean theorem.... And, I think they're so ready to get it when they are little kids.... I think that as soon as they get to high school, if that seed hasn't been planted, there's not much hope. But, as adults, I think that we become very cynical, and we think, well that will never change, that's just the way it is, you just have to get over it.... And so, I think it's important to sort of start early, because little kids get it. They get fair.

◎ Mindy: Blake and the Laramie Project

You know what... If we're going to talk about Laramie Project, * *it's long, and it's probably more tape then you need, so I'm just going to warn you... because you need to hear the whole story. Because it is a combination of teacher, and theatre, and politics.*

The story starts in 2001, and I had this charming, delightful, drug addicted, failing, young boy in my class [named Blake], and he was absolutely a delight, and I couldn't understand why he was abusing himself so much. He seemed to have everything going for him, looks and talent. So, I got him involved with theatre. Little by little all the problems didn't stop, at all. But, we developed a fairly strong rapport... and we started talking about the drugs, quite honestly... . He wanted to TA for my class. Well, I said, I can't have you TA... the drugs are a problem if the kids know about it, so he did his best, and he would keep me up to date on the drugs.... A new school year started, and he did TA, and... we did a lot of theatre together. One day... at the beginning of class, he was looking soooo—depressed and sad, and I said, "Are you okay," and he said, "No, not really." And he said, "Can I talk to you after school?" And I said, "Sure." So we agreed, he went out, he had his smoke, and, we agreed to meet in the portable.

So I sat and waited for him, and he «burst» through the door, and he said, "You know I'm gay, right?" and I said, "Well... I swear, I haven't really thought about it, but I guess it doesn't surprise me...." So, we sat for the longest time, because he had just been outed, and he ran with... a very tough, really tough druggy group, and he's like—"I'm dead"— this is how he felt. And... it got late; I took him home. His mom knew, his father didn't. He contacted me via email again, wanted to continue the discussion. And, email is always a grey area... with a young male student and a teacher, but it seemed to be really important. So, we went for coffee... for five hours. And we just sat and talked, and talked and talked, and talked.

I had to keep a really good eye on him, I kept peeping in his classroom to see if he was there, because I really thought he was going to hurt himself. As it turns out, he hadn't been outed.... But, it struck me that this kid was living in fear... because he was so closeted, and... you didn't

---

* The *Laramie Project* is a play by Moises Kaufman. Kaufman and his theatre troupe developed the play from interviews with community members in Laramie, Wyoming following the hate crime that led to the death of Matthew Sheppard, a young gay man.

have to be a brain surgeon to, all of a sudden, realize that there was a connection with the drugs, and there was a connection with the school, and all sorts of things...

That story goes on for quite some time, but at the end of that year, we had been given some money to do some workshops. I was able to take a group of kids to Laketown, and workshop with these American playwrights who came up, and we did some great work. During that time... one by one, he took the girls out on the porch, and came out, sort of individually. I had picked up a copy of The Laramie Project, and I said to him on the trip, read this, and let me know what you think. And he was so—so touched by it. And I said, "I think that I've gotta do this. It's a tough play, but I think I really, really feel that we need to do this."

So, it was a new principal, and... he had heard me speak at the last staff meeting about the language in the halls, and my speech was pretty rough, I mean I stood up and said we don't use nigger, chick, spick in the hall, and you don't allow it... so, why are you allowing the following language... [Here, I assume Mindy to be referring to homophobic slurs]. *He was really impressed; I didn't know he came from a really socially activist background. So, at the beginning of the year, I went to him, and I handed him the Laramie Project, and I said, "How much do you like your job?"* [Mindy laughs] *And if you meet with him, he will talk about that.* * *And I said, "Read this." And, he came back from the weekend, and he just sort of, and his eyes were really wide and he went "Okay."*

We had been told [by administrative powers beyond the school] that we could not do the Laramie Project. It was too mature, or it was too risqué. And... A problem arose in that a local theatre was doing a professional production of it, so we weren't allowed the rights. But, we continued to rehearse anyway. We did it at my house, we did it on site after school hours, six to ten... not knowing if we'd ever be able to get the show up on the road. One of the great stories from Laramie is how great these kids were, I had 15 of them, doing 120 parts, and, my young boy, Blake who really wanted to complete his coming out process but was having a hard time with it. But he was in this play... and so he made a comment backstage one night that another one of the actors took as being homophobic, and started an altercation with him {Blake}, and said "Has

---

* Mindy connected me with her former principal, Dave. One of his stories is shared in chapter three.

this play taught you nothing?" And, so, here was this young gay male who was just accused of being a homophobe, you know, being an actor in the Laramie Project. And, he came to me and he said, "He think's I'm a homophobe." And I'm like this is the perfect opportunity for you to do something. He didn't, at that time.

A week later on Valentine's day, his father found out he was gay and threw him out of the house. He showed up at my doorstep.... On Valentine's day. So, we chatted. We chatted until like 7 o'clock in the morning, when he decided he was brave enough to go home. That was really an unpleasant thing. It gave him enough courage, though, to, when we were having a cast meeting, very casually to say, "Ya, I understand all these issues. Ya, my dad just found out I'm gay and he threw me out of the house, so..." And, and then that was it.

So... two weeks before we were to open, we got the rights to the actual play, so we were able to stage it at Riverside. We had been building and everything all along.... The principal felt for our personal safety... so, he asked that we not extensively advertise outside the school, which was his moment of caution. And, the guy had been so brave already, that, alright... so, I ended up with his cell phone number to call in emergency—I mean, over a play, and a bunch of high school kids. But he was... I mean, he was right, because Jack Layton High School did it a few years ago, and there was a huge threat of you know, Fred Phelps and the Westboro Baptist Church showing up to protest outside of it. We ran six shows, we were tremendously successful, we were sold out... Blake's father came to the show, and I think that the actual performance really had an impact on Dad.

So, that was our Laramie Project, and it had a tremendous effect on the kids that were in the production and a lot of the people who came to see it. Mostly you are preaching to the converted anyway, when you do a piece like The Laramie Project... But, you also get family members and stuff who really don't know what's going on, who sit there and listen to those words, and listen to, you know... One of the characters, one of the actors, Jedidiah, his mother doesn't want to come see him in a "gay play," and he's like, "Mom, I played Macbeth last night... I killed people on stage." It just made so much sense.... And, Moises Kaufman, at the introduction of The Laramie Project talks about Burtolt Brecht, and the concept of... Brechtian theatre—where you are actually meant to think, not to feel.... The feeling sort of comes later. And, that was certainly the impact of our play.

And, so after doing The Laramie Project, and using that structure, I think I'm better at… social pieces like that…. Anyway… I mean, Matthew Shepard died in 1998, and I can remember taking it in to a… drama class, at the time, and… just, being so devastated… about the protest… in front of his parents. I think that piece of history… I think that moment… would probably be the moment that I became the cranky old woman who talked about what's wrong with the world.

ⓒ Colleen: The Act of Educating is an Act of Activism

I think there's doing education in a way that engages you and your students in other social issues, other activist projects… so, taking education into activism…. But, I think education itself can be looked at as activism, if as a teacher you are trying… an approach to learning and to schooling that moves toward something more democratic, something where students have some self-determination…. I would say that I would probably identify a lot more with the side of… doing activism in education. The act of educating is an act of activism.

I think if you're curious about something, and it compels you to get to know that "other," whether that other is… a plant or a tree, or a person… whatever it is. Then, when you get to know that other entity… then I think that leads to more of a sense of care. You know, the opposite would be sort of an apathy and disinterest in the world, and… remaining fairly ignorant about things and people that are different from you and therefore not really caring.

I think what happens through a self-directed learning experience like that is that the care the students feel becomes their own. I didn't indoctrinate them into caring about a particular issue. They… came to care about whatever it was that they were learning about and whoever they were interacting with because of their own interest. And so, it's kind of authentic, and… maybe they'll end up caring about some similar things to me, but it wasn't because I planted… it ultimately wasn't because I planted that.

I think it's quite important to make it possible for students to… feel connected to a larger community, to people of different generations, to people doing different sorts of jobs, to people who are making different sorts of contributions to the community. Learning from experience is quite important…. So… keeping a… broader natural world connected to education and learning and schooling is important to me.

I think if education can… compel students to become active citizens, and they make a choice about how they want to spend their energy and their time, then that's… exciting too. It would be very difficult as a teacher to… teach a curriculum that you disbelieved… and, I don't think it's necessarily wrong that your opinion gets in there…. But, helping students understand that there is a situatedness to things, and that people have an identity, and people have biases is important. You can't remove your personal commitments and your personal beliefs from what you're doing, and I think it's not authentic if you try. I don't think it's even possible to try. So, I think being transparent about it, and talking about how your positionality influences what's going on in the classroom. And, I think talking about that with students, and helping the students figure out what some of their beliefs are, and how their beliefs, you know, influence the way they're interacting in the classroom.

PRAXIS POINTS
Learning Activities for Exploring Social Justice Ideas

Activity❧ Kite Running: Exploring Globalization

This reflection and experiential object lesson is contributed by Peter Mullins, a seasoned English teacher at the high school level in Ontario, Canada. His example arises from his experience teaching literature in the International Baccalaureate Diploma program. *The Kite Runner* explores social justice issues surrounding ethnicity, social class, and forced migration, among others (Kemchandani-Daswani, n.d.). Teachers and students can engage with the story through the original novel (Hosseini, 2004) or the film adaptation (Forster, 2007). Peter's debriefing of the experience with students draws out social justice principles around equity and challenging privilege and oppression. An excerpt from Peter's social justice journal offers a sense of what the lesson means for him, and may mean for his students:

> I am teaching *The Kite Runner* by Khaled Hosseini (2004), set in Afghanistan during the rise of the Taliban. To honour the cultural tradition of kite running, we make kites to fly on the back field…. Later, we discuss themes: Islamic fundamentalism, displacement of minority groups, the protracted challenges of the post-colonial experience. Building this lesson is challenging. With Taliban violence having permeated the news and recently the Pulse Nightclub mass shooting in Orlando, I recognize this lesson may make Muslim students uneasy. Equally, how will non-Muslim students react given

the sensitive nature of this material? Moreover, what assumptions have I made about places and processes—particularly colonialism—which neither I, nor many of my students, have seen, smelled or tasted, let alone felt? How does Afghanistan live in my students' minds; or in mine? Which Afghanistan will we discuss? Whose?

The students shift in their seats as our discussion concludes. What do I make of their silence? Are they affirmed? Reflecting on new tendrils of learning? Does the safe flight of our kites—kite running was banned by the Taliban—act as a form of resistance, or are we voyeurs irrevocably compromised by privilege?

The Lesson

This activity and subsequent discussion is an object lesson in which participants have a live experience with a kite, a significant metaphoric symbol in *The Kite Runner* and a cherished cultural practice in Afghanistan where the novel is set. This lesson is intended to be delivered as a culminating task after having read the whole novel or having viewed the film.

Materials

- Doweling, or bamboo stakes
- Strong thin twine or string
- Strong paper or other lightweight material for the sail
- Tape and/or glue
- Markers, paint, or other supplies for decorating

Note: If your context doesn't permit making and decorating kites, inexpensive prefabricated kite kits may be purchased for the activity.

Minds On

Screen one or more videos to show participants what kite fighting and kite running look like in Afghan culture. At the time of publication, these videos on YouTube.com offer effective illustration:

› *Afghanistan – The Toughest Battle – Kite Running – 14 May 07* (Al Jezeera English, 2007)
› *Viewfinder: The Real Kite Runners* (HDNetWorldReport, 2011)
› *Fly Kites Not Drones in Afghanistan* (Our Journey to Smile, 2014)

Action!

Construct your kite

- Lash two lengths of doweling together to form an uneven cross.

- Stretch a length of string around the four points of the diamond shaped kite frame, to help maintain its shape.
- Cut the sail material slightly larger than the frame of the kite, to allow for folding the sail around the outside of the kite frame.
- With the edges of the sail folded around the frame, glue or tape the sail into place.
- Secure a loose length of string from the tip to the tail of the kite frame, by which to attach the kite's flying line. Attach the flying line with a secure knot, and wind excess line around an object that will serve as the kite's reel. (Instructions adapted, in brief, from Jen at www.sketch-pad.com/kites/make.html)

Fly your kite!
- Allow participants several minutes for free practice with their kites.
- Engage in a competition like those described in the kite runner and seen in the videos.

Note: Working with glass powder to coat kite strings as in the novel is beyond the skill and comfort level of most North American teachers and students and presents risk management concerns. Consider other friendly competition ideas to develop community amongst participants (e.g., highest kite, longest flying time, etc.)

Questions for Reflection
- How did it feel to make and fly your own kite with your peers? How might this be different than the ways you usually recreate together?
- Describe a joyful or other positive moment that you experienced while flying your kite. Did you experience any frustrations?
- How would you feel if your government decided that you and your community were no longer allowed to fly kites? Is there a cherished activity in your local community? How would you react to its prohibition?
- The story of *The Kite Runner* shows many ways that people in a society can experience inequity or privilege and oppression. What aspects of privilege and oppression do you notice most in the story? How do these inequities compare (or contrast?) with inequities in our country or community?
- How might kite flying help to overcome this social challenge for the story's characters? For us? Are there cultural practices in our own communities that challenge privilege and oppression?

Extensions

• Through its human rights education program, Amnesty International offers a curriculum supplement for *The Kite Runner* that takes a strong social justice approach to the novel (Kemchandani-Daswani, n.d.).

• flykitesnotdrones.org offers a series of learning activity outlines (both workshops and larger assemblies) that extend the themes of *The Kite Runner* around contemporary issues related to global relations and drone warfare in Afghanistan and elsewhere outside the western world (attacks by unmanned, armed aircraft), positioning the kite as a symbol of hope for people whose lives are perpetually under attack.

Activity⁂ Colour Blind Initiative: Exploring Gender Norms

This activity framing taps into social justice ideas around gender, in particular around the association of a loud or commanding voice with masculinity and power. This gender-focused framing of the colour blind initiative was initially published as Niblett & Potvin (2010). "Colourblind" was created by Elite Training (n.d.).

Materials

• A set of colour coded shapes, with one shape in each of a variety of colours. Shape sets can be purchased from a variety of experiential education vendors, or can be cut from craft foam.

• Blindfolds (or participants can just close their eyes)

The Challenge

The group must work together to identify by shape and colour which two pieces have been removed from the shape set by the facilitator. Participants will be unsighted (eyes closed or blindfolded), and may not touch shapes assigned to other participants or allow others to touch the shapes assigned to them. The facilitator provides unlimited correct responses to the question, "What colour is this?" but will otherwise remain silent.

Typical Framing Script

This activity is called "colour blind" and once we get started, I think you will see why. The central focus of the activity is a set of coloured shapes; the shapes come in an array of colours, but there are only one of each shape in each colour. A few moments ago, I removed two shapes from the set. The group's task is to discover which two shapes are missing and what colour they are. In a moment, I'll ask everyone to put a blindfold over their eyes (or to simply close their eyes if they prefer), and then I'll pass out the shapes. Each person will be given one or two shapes, and you will need to hang onto your own shapes during the entire activity—you can't give any of your shapes to anyone, nor may anyone touch any of your shapes. Everyone will be blindfolded, so nobody will be able to see what coloured shapes they are holding. Once we begin, you may all talk as much as you like, but I will only answer the question, "What colour is this?" If anyone has questions about the activity instructions, please ask them now.

Important Points

- Between 20 and 50 minutes are needed to complete the activity, depending on the group.
- The initial minutes of the activity typically look and sound quite chaotic. The degree of the chaos depends on group maturity, experience working together, stage of the program, and clarity of instructions given.
- Depending on the desired challenge level for the activity, the facilitator can adjust the degree of detail given in the briefing. If the group is functioning at a high level, it may not be necessary to spell out that the shapes form a patterned set; it may be enough to say there are 2 shapes missing, and they need to figure out which ones.
- Ensure that the 2 shapes are removed from the set (I usually place them discretely in my pocket). It is easy enough to forget, and doing so ruins the ideal outcome of the activity, and may create unwanted tension between the group and facilitator.

Questions for Reflection

- What are some words that characterize the behaviour of our group during the activity and our feelings about what was happening? (It may be helpful to record this group brainstorm on a board or flipchart.)

- How would you attribute gender to the behaviours and feelings that we have brainstormed? Which are traditionally considered masculine or feminine?
- Which of these behaviours enabled a player to participate most in the group's problem solving process? Which led to the most success in problem solving?
- Did anyone engage in behaviours that were attributed to a gender other than their own identified gender? If so, why do you think this may have happened?

Reflection Notes
- Deep reflection of the gender dynamics of the activity may require time away. Consider brainstorming an initial list of behaviours and feelings right after the activity, and coming back to further questions about gender at a later time.
- Avoid polarizing judgments when discussing gendered behaviours in the activity (e.g., shouting=masculine=bad, quiet cooperation=feminine=good). Instead, try to focus discussion on the complexity of gender norms and relations that may have emerged during the activity.
- While the intention here is to generate discussion about gender norms, teaching and learning through initiative tasks can be unpredictable. Avoid forcing a discussion of gender norms where the outcome of the activity doesn't warrant it. At the same time, also be aware that some participants (of all genders) may be reluctant to name gender privilege even when it seems obvious to others.

CHAPTER ⑤ SOCIAL JUSTICE EDUCATION IN ACTIONS

The actions element of social justice education is described as a series of **doings** in chapter two—behaviours that have complex connections to the element of ideas as discussed in chapter four. Here, these connections are highlighted as teachers tell stories of the actions they take to work toward social justice principles with students through formal curriculum delivery and in extracurricular contexts.

As readers engage with teachers' stories around social justice actions, take note of connections to those from chapter four—even when stories are told by different tellers. For instance, consider the relationship between Mindy's account of her principal's trepidation about approving a school production of *The Laramie Project* in chapter four and Andrea's description in this chapter of the cautionary permission granted by her administrator for the school hosting the first Day of Pink. Likewise, Jennifer talks about critical thinking as a process of learning being more important than specific required content, which seems to resonate with Colleen's narrative in this chapter about developing curiosity and self-directedness as learner dispositions through an outdoor adventure learning experience. These, and other points of connection, serve to illustrate the depth of relationship between the ideas that support social justice and the actions that bring those ideas into reality. Although the two elements go hand-in-hand, most would agree there is something crucially different between teaching about a particular social justice idea and facilitating processes through which students have opportunities to enact that idea to affect positive change.

The stories shared in this chapter highlight some of the many possible actions teachers and students can take to bring social justice ethics to life in their learning environments. The exemplars run the spectrum from politically charged to relatively inert (remembering my position from chapter one that no education is ever politically neutral), but each story illustrates a gesture toward Freire's keystone concept of **concientizacion**, where education is a process aimed at leading both educators and learners toward more compassionate humanity driven by the belief that each person has some ability to act as an agent of that humanity.

The key social justice principle of fostering agency and action suggests a strong connection between social justice actions and an individual's or group's agency. As seen in the upcoming stories, actions in support of social justice are both an outcome of actors' agency and a means of helping those actors renew their sense and understanding of their own ability to play a part in shaping their communities.

IN THEIR OWN WORDS...

ⓒ Andrea: This Has to Be Deepened!

I can't remember if it was my second year teaching, or my third year. I think it was my second year teaching. I had a student... she was part of an extra-curricular group that I was supervising... So, I'm teaching this girl... But it turns out, and I know this just through being part of this community, that her eldest brother is gay. And, so she comes to me and she says, "You know, I've heard about these Gay/Straight Alliance {GSA} things, and I'd really like to start one, and would you be interested in, you know, being the supervisor"—absolutely! So, that to me felt really good... to look back and know that it came from a student....

So, I'm helping and guiding the students that want this GSA, and like there's four of them, or three of them... not a lot of them, but they're dedicated.... They're working hard, to do the first pink shirt day.* And, it was the first pink shirt day that I'm pretty sure had been done in the city. And... the school that I was working in had a human rights complaint against it by a former student, for homophobic bullying and harassment.... So, I like, knew I could be up against something here. I remember a very important conversation happening with my vice-principal at

---

* Pink Shirt day, or Day of Pink is a campaign against homophobic bullying in schools. For background on the event, visit http://www.dayofpink.org

the time, and that was a crossroads for me. Like, I made a decision from then on that this was the path that I was taking in terms of activism, and if the school board wasn't ready for it, or if there were repercussions for me because of it, then, there would be repercussions and I would take them... like, negative repercussions, right? So, I said to her {the vice-principal}, "You know, I want to do, we want to do this pink shirt day... So... she said, "Well, you just need to be aware of what you're biting off here, and there might be repercussions." And, like, the tone of the conversation was like—back off, don't do this. And, I was like, well, we're gonna do it and see what happens. And, I was given permission to do it, but it was sort of like, with this cautionary tone. And, thank god there's a strong teacher's union, because that gives you the security that as long as you're dotting your i's and crossing your t's, they've got your back.

But, I spent a lot of time, of course, reflecting on how authentic that participation {in pink shirt day} was.... The fact that we, and by we I mean myself and the students in the GSA, were encouraging people to wear pink to take a stand against homophobic harassment in schools... Now, of course, I think that having one-off shirt days isn't the be all and end all. I know... with the GSAs, that I was working to... deepen the conversation.... I think it was Greg... one of my students who I had... power struggles with. He was wearing pink on pink day, and then in my classroom was making super homophobic comments... They were envisioning an island... it was a civics class, and they were envisioning what the rules of the island would be, a la Lord of the Flies.... One of his rules would be that no gay people would be allowed.... And, the kids in the class were like, "Dude, it's pink day, and you're wearing pink, and you're saying homophobic stuff... like, what are you doing?" And, he was like "Well, I'm just wearing this because everyone else is wearing pink."

And that for me was a moment as an activist educator where I was like, "Oh my god, like, I've failed.... I'VE FAILED!" I failed because this kid, like, I'm feeling all happy, everyone's wearing pink, and like, the boys get super flamboyant.... They've got streamers tied to them, and like boas, and like every boy with some kind of closeted issues decides that he's going to dress in drag for the day, you know.... But, this kid was like... wearing the pink, and saying homophobic things. So, I think that for me was a moment in time where I was like, this has to be deepened.

So, then it continued... we were going to have a week of events, or something to do with international anti-homophobia day. And the kids wanted to have a march. There was another school, and they had like made this beautiful, hand painted GSA banner for like, a march. And, *basically we were going to walk like two blocks down the street, two blocks back, and have a potluck and a presentation by the local LGBTQ advocacy group. At the school. And, a superintendent heard, I don't, I can't remember which word was the problem…. It was like a walk/demonstration/march…. I didn't know which would be most acceptable to the institution. Well, it turns out that none of them were, and they were afraid, that of course, it would be bad press for the board. And, as soon as the word "demonstration" was made, it was shut down. I was, we were told we could not do it, there would be no demonstrations.*

Before my last year… myself and the other teacher running the GSA did a workshop for the staff. About homophobia in schools…. But, teachers were like, "Well, I don't know how to deal with this…. I don't want to talk about sex with my students." It isn't about sex! So anyway, we had a wonderful, meaningful workshop with staff, and people that you would not expect were coming up… after and saying, "You know what, like, I heard a kid saying 'that's so gay' in the hallway, and… I knew what to say because of your workshop" So… holy shit, that's awesome!… So, you go from kid-wearing-pink being homophobic, 3-years later doing a staff workshop, with, this is the same staff that… I was told was… not going to respond well to pink shirt day, and they're like, "Just give us the tools… just give us the tools." And I think that maybe that's a big, huge piece of activism for me too, is like, you provide the tools. So many people… have dissenting voices, or a voice of dissent about something, but then they don't know how to make that voice heard. What are the productive ways to dissent…? How can you be a dissenting voice in a high school environment, whether you're a student or a teacher?

So…. this particular author… Jennifer Tupper (2005)… she's influenced by Michael Apple quite heavily…. the notion of being disruptive, or "interrupting" the moment. And, I am an interrupter of the highest order. But, her concept is… it's very important that we interrupt the dominant narrative for those critical questions. And, kids are great at interrupting the dominant narrative, and asking those questions. And, we're really quick as educators, to try to stick to our lesson plans, and to our timelines…. But there's a lot of richness in those interruptions, and for me that became, in my sort of quest, a way to do activism ethically in the classroom. Or… for my own satisfaction, to not feel like I was imposing my values on students, I encourage the questioning and encourage the interruptions. And, I felt like that… was a way that I could sort of reconcile those—the relationship between activism and education.

ⓖ Colleen: Cross Country Curiosity

So, okay, we've loaded up a 15 passenger white van with 12 students, and.... One of the 5 courses that students were taking was... Canadian history, culture and identity, and we thought that if we spent 3 weeks driving across the country and back, that would be a good experiential way to think about Canadian identity.... And, the funny thing is, that to me... my most significant teaching has been in these alternative sorts of situations, so it's kind of become the norm, so although they're all incredible and amazing, it sort of seems normal. There were so many moments... we visited the mint, we stopped in a farmer's field in Saskatchewan, we... paddled outside of Vancouver Island, we... stopped in a park and met with a Canadian artist who was on tour across Canada. We... spent so many hours a day listening to CBC radio and having discussions about it. We had... two vehicle breakdowns.

But, I think, you know, each of those little moments were not that different, they were just fairly regular moments you'd have, that anyone who was going traveling would have.... But, I think what happened overall is... the students saw that... this wasn't just the next history project. That learning about Canada's history, learning about... you know, what multiplicities of identities there are in Canada, and having these conversations doesn't have to end—because, it's actually really interesting, and they can continue to live their life and to interact with the world in that way if that inspires them.

I mean I don't know that they learned more about Canada... but, I think that they learned more about themselves as learners.... So, fostering that self-directedness, fostering that sense of curiosity in the larger community.... learning how to ask questions... it was never really about the content. So, I think that's maybe how the experience is different. But, at the same time, it's not different. I mean, when people take a year off from school and go traveling, they do often change as people, and they do often become engaged in the world.

So, what was our role as educators, or as facilitators? How did it make it educational...? I've had students, and other people that I've worked with tell me that a big role of mine on those trips was... to foster that curiosity. They would just be astounded at how excited I would get at things, and they would laugh. At the beginning, they would laugh at me that I would go up to the guy on the park bench and ask him a question, or that I would roll down my window at a stop sign and knock on the truck next door.... For example, we were driving in Montreal, and

I don't have a clue what the question was, but the students had asked a question in the van, and we became curious about something, and we happened to stop at a stoplight, and I thought, well, I'll just ask the guy. And, they were in total disbelief, that you could just do that. You know, that you could have a conversation with him. But then, you would notice that they would start to do it as well. And, you know, some of the students in that class, I've been able to continue to know, and they've continued to live their lives that way. They've continued to take advantage of learning from the people around them.... For example, they won't be satisfied with just the discussion in class, or the reading.... But, they'll... take the time to stop somewhere on their way home because they think that person might contribute something to the discussion. So that is, to me, really amazing.

Another project that we used to get involved with, was... hiking on the Big Bay Hiking Trail, ... Leading up to it, we would study... two... environmental controversies that were taking place there. One was they wanted to build a liquefied natural gas terminal... in this small town of Baysdale, and the entire community of Baysdale was talking about you know stereotypical activism. There were posters everywhere, there were protests, there were rallies in the gyms, there were speeches by politicians [Right.]. And, we would kind of start learning about this issue, and then when we got there, we had preplanned meetings with different people. So... the other environmental issue we were looking at was aquaculture, so we had meetings with a local biologist, with the local whale watching tourism operator, with the local high school students, with, uh, the local chief of {a First Nation}.... And then, we went and sat in Tim Horton's and had our discussions. And the people around us noticed that we were this class visiting, that we were having these discussions, and... the retired man at that table... joined into our discussion.... The students were fascinated that they could see that this issue that had originally just been something that we were studying by reading articles,—we were trying to give them some background before we went out east, and it was usually a little bit like pulling teeth. It was when we got there and the students could see that this was a really central issue in these people's lives, then they became curious, and they cared about the people in that community.

ⓒ Grace: The Green Team

The green team... is our school's environmental club.... Everyone that's in that group has a passion to make change... I think, like, the group does, there's some annual events, they do the twenty-minute make-

over, they do gardening around the school… they have campaigns after doing a waste audit, depending on what is like most problematic that year, to try and raise awareness in the school. And, then they try and work on the eco-schools goals to make sure that the school retains its silver certification. So, that involves a lot of awareness about energy conservation and waste minimization, and I'd say the biggest challenge is to try to meet the goals of eco-schools while meeting the interests of the kids. Because sometimes what you can do to make the school the most sustainable can be just a bunch of checklists that you've made sure you've accomplished. And that doesn't necessarily lead to the most creative, inspiring actions. So, the other thing that we try and do is like, have events throughout the year that are special to the Green Team. Like, going on a big hike, or going to an outdoor-education centre.

[Would you say that the action is primarily driven by the students, or driven by staff?] *So, right now, this year, sooo by me. And that's the part where I feel like I'm not being a successful leader of the group. Cuz, you know, I'm working on the binder tonight for our audit. And, I'm figuring out what we can do for this meeting tomorrow, but it's not them. And, there's been a few events where they've got the chance to shine, but, no… I'm carrying the group right now.…*

Sometimes kids are in a bunch of groups because they want to be involved in the school, but sometimes they just want to have a ticket… you know, it's good for your resume.… So there are those things… and I work at a school where the students aren't natural leaders as much. The reason I can say that is because when I was at Downtown Collegiate, students ran the eco-team.… They had an executive… and they involved outside parties, and they fundraised, and it was amazing to be in the background of that. I was only an observer in that place, and it was amazing and inspiring. Because that's what you want in the end. So, there's that; but then, at Frankwood Collegiate you have to start everything. And there's a lot more energy that goes into that.… The culture is younger. And, I would say that's the biggest factor… it's a younger school.

ⓒ Tim: Activist Trigonometry (or, Institutionalizing Community-Based Environmental Justice Education)

Activist education can be… really challenging for educators who have no background, but it need not be. And, some of the exciting things that I see, to give you an example of less obvious roots.… There is a movement in North America… mainly in the States… where school districts or schools, where individual teachers are checking with public authorities to see what studies need to be done that the public authorities don't have money for. And... now there are towns in New England and the Pacific Northwest states where the town manager doesn't award a contract to an engineering firm to do a project until they've thought about which part of the project the kids in the neighbouring schools can do.

A grade 11 math teacher in a little place called Seaside, Oregon, a community that at the time was a bit preoccupied by the potentially destructive forces of a tsunami wave that once in 50 years would... be magnified as it funneled up their inlet to their town at the top of that inlet. And... and they had decided they couldn't afford a $700,000 study that would look at the impact of a magnified tsunami wave on the buildings along the sea wall in their town. And, this teacher got wind of this and said, well this is a perfect project for my grade 11 trigonometry class. And, got the permission of her school district to be absolved of state curriculum for the following year so that they could work on this project. And, they took it up, and of course as the kids took up the project, and started using their trigonometry skills learned during the course, they then started realizing that, you know, they needed to do some public education about all of this... And so they... developed public display boards to be mounted along the boardwalk on the sea wall, but also made presentations to the town council.... So, they were doing art for these displays, and they were doing language arts as well... developing... persuasive arguments... about what they thought should happen, what the town should do as a result of their findings. And, of course, here are grade 11 kids who were incredibly motivated the whole year, learning far more effectively because they were. If... one was to do objective tests, they probably did better on their standardized tests, and all that other bullshit that matters to traditional educators. But, it also meant that they were far more engaged, and they probably learned a lot about subjects that they previously didn't care about... because they needed those skills to be effective change agents in their communities.

You know, the traditional side of activist education is the lone teacher who... either is personally inspired and motivated on a particular issue, and shares that with their kids... or the kids themselves come up with an idea that they want to do something on an issue after talking... about current events, and stuff like that. And, it's really challenging for individual teachers; sometimes they only do it if they can get enough support from their administrator. But often they don't, and they're frustrated, and they have to kind of, it's just a difficult thing to navigate through in a sys-

tem that's... designed to keep kids within the four walls of the building—and, studying, you know, their Ps and Qs.

And, so, I look for things that can institutionalize. How do you transform education in ways that are going to enable kids... and enable teachers more easily to do this? Instead of schools just being... accidentally located in the middle of each neighbourhood... They would become much more valued by the whole community, because it's the whole community that is impacted by students that are taking up projects that are of value... or taking stands on issues, and educating their communities.... Kids have to be involved with their communities—to develop citizenship skills, but also because of what we know about brain-based learning. Kids sitting in rows regurgitating stuff does not take advantage of their brains.... Attention drives emotion, and emotion drives learning, and... it's hands-on community projects that engage you. And, so that alone is a compelling argument that propels us toward a more engaged kind of educational process—a more activist process.

PRAXIS POINTS
Learning Activities Social Justice Action

Activity❧ Privilege Treasure Hunt

Adapted from Fawcett, Bell, & Russell (2002), with thanks to Connie Russell

Overview

One of the biggest challenges of social justice education work is helping students to see privilege and oppression in their day-to-day lives. The common and pervasive nature of privilege means it can often be invisible in plain sight; relations of privilege and oppression can be so familiar that people hardly take notice of them.

Privilege is a deeply complex concept that can be as basic as fairness or as complex as hegemony (the invisible social and cultural assumptions that often go unquestioned in our lives). Thus, privilege as a concept for learning may be considered low floor, high ceiling (Boaler, 2016), meaning it can be discussed at many levels of complexity.

In this exercise, participants work in pairs or small groups to walk around their learning environment or its larger community and identify elements of privilege. I offer framings of a treasure hunt activity for groups at three different levels of development. The exercise is intended to follow a group discussion on privilege that will help students focus their treasure hunt based on their understanding of what privilege means.

Materials
- Clipboards, paper, and writing instruments for recording treasure hunt findings
- Alternatively, participants may use digital cameras, or mobile digital devices to document their findings.

Three Framings for Age/Development Groups

Primary Years
As we go on a walk as a group, I'd like you to look around for things that our school and/or community thinks are important. How can you tell that they are important? How are they different from other things that may be less important to our community?

Middle Years
Walk with a partner for five minutes and see how many examples or symbols of fairness or unfairness you notice as you travel. Use your senses to observe (look, listen, smell, feel).

Young Adult/Adult Education
Alone or with a small group, walk for ten minutes in the school/ community in search of examples of the main cultural assumptions of our community (e.g., things members of our community generally assume about our relationships with one another). What things do these assumptions privilege? What things are not assigned privilege, or are marginalized?

Further Considerations
This activity can be easily integrated into the following community mapping exercise.

Questions for Reflection
- What did you find when you went looking for examples of privilege in our school and community?
- Do the examples that we have selected show privileging and "othering" in our school or community? If so, how so?
- Using one of our found examples, how does the privilege that some people experience affect people who don't share that experience of privilege?

- If an example of privilege creates unfairness for some people, how can we speak or act in order to effectively work toward fairness in relation to that example?

Activity⟋ Social Justice Mapping

Maps can be powerful social justice tools, not only because they can depict issues of social justice and injustice in visually impactful ways, but also because they can be created by anybody. The process of making maps can build community, foster agency and action, promote equity and challenge privilege and oppression (the principles of social justice education described in chapter one).

Various names have been used to describe mapping movements that promote social justice ends, including community mapping (Mears, 2012), participatory mapping (Rainforest Foundation UK, 2011), and barefoot mapping (Hoffman & Jones, 2001). This exercise blends these approaches into a mapping exercise that can be adapted for use to explore a range of social justice issues across a variety of educational contexts.

Background Principles

Some key ideas underpin the process of community mapping (adapted from Rainforest Foundation UK, 2011):

- Community mapping is an inclusive process. The more people who have input into the boundaries and features of a community map, the more people who will feel the map is a useful representation of their spatial lives.
- Maps produced through community mapping belong to that community and can be used to share its stories and aspirations; they can convey community agency at broader regional and national levels.
- Community maps emphasize the value of local knowledge of a place and how it is inhabited and used.
- Community mappers are aware of, but not bound by rules of formal mapping. Formal conventions may be used insofar as they aid in telling the story that the community wants to tell through the map, but can be altered or abandoned if they hinder the community's need to construct their map in particular ways.

The Mapping Process

Developing an effective community map is a detailed procedure, which would take a whole chapter or more to communicate. Here I outline, in broad strokes, possible phases of community map production with a focus on social and ecological justice and point to some other resources for more detailed instructions. These phases are adapted from Hoffman and Jones (2001), and Mears (2012).

Preparation: Learning and Getting Ready to Map

- **Opportunities and problems:** What makes you care about the chosen space? What key ideas about your chosen space will the map convey? How will your map help make the mapped area a better space for the people and more-than human occupants of the area?
- **Understanding key mapping concepts (e.g., scale, legend, base map, transect, etc.):** This opens up an opportunity for skill building and cross-curricular learning.

Mapping in Action: Gathering Detailed Information

- **Technical tasks:** Establish a base map (an outline on which features can be plotted), orient the map to north, and establish scale and grid (if you want your map to reflect these mapping conventions).
- **Physical data collection:** Closely observe and record features and conditions found in the mapping area (could include above ground, on the ground, and under the ground).
- **Social data collection:** Converse with and observe the people who use the space being mapped. Record their ideas, feelings, and thoughts about what the space means to them. This may include interviews, photographs, drawings, paintings, dances. The sky is the limit!

Map Assembly and Sharing

- **Integration of data collection findings with the base map:** The mapper's now extensive knowledge of the space is integrated onto the base map. This may involve drawing, painting, digital technologies, or 2D/3D extensions (e.g., pins/tape/string for connecting photographs or collection samples with a point on the map).

- **Sharing:** Share the map with others to highlight the care the mappers have for the space and the agency sparked by this care. Use the community map as a tool for advocating for positive change in the community.

Further Considerations

- Community maps can take many physical forms, from traditional paper maps, to painted canvases, to complex digital renderings using geographic information system (GIS) technology, to performance art. No matter the medium of presentation, the process of community-based inquiry remains the foundation of a community map.
- Consider integrating a community mapping exercise with the privilege treasure hunt activity previously described.

Questions for Reflection

- What was the most significant learning you had in making the community map? Did you have an "ah-ha!" moment at some point in the process?
- How do you think about the space after participating in the community mapping? Is this different than before?
- What positive changes can our community map have for the space that we have mapped together?
- How can we continue to act in support of this community, either by using our map as a tool, or in other ways?

AN OUTRODUCTION

As I begin this ending chapter, I cannot help but contemplate the nature of beginnings and endings, their role in stories and in the quest for understanding that constitutes teaching and learning. Stories are at the heart of this book. Indeed, the heart of social justice education lies in the stories people tell about equity, challenging privilege and oppression, building community, and fostering agency and action. Throughout the previous three chapters, teachers have shared their experiences in thinking about and enacting social justice through their classroom practices. In this chapter, I offer some trends and opportunities that resonate across the narratives. I begin with a story of my own.

In the week before sitting down to write this chapter, I attended an event with friends and colleagues hosted by my university. During a break in the program, I turned to my friend, Sandra, who is an elementary school teacher with strong and deep social justice commitments.

"How have you been?" I asked her, having not seen her in several months.

"It's hard, Blair. It's really hard." Tears welled up in Sandra's eyes as she described how difficult it felt to carry the burden of self-identification as a social justice educator.

She told me how overwhelming and disheartening it can be, completing all the work that is expected as the "basics" of teaching (essential curriculum delivery, supporting student learning, staff meetings, parent meetings, collecting and organizing lunch moneys and other forms, etc.), plus doing this within the context of environments, ideas, and actions that support anti-oppressive social change. She talked about how difficult it was to find support, both from within the school where she works and in the larger, formal and informal education networks. She also asked me pointedly, but not accusingly, about the role of the university school of education in promoting and supporting social justice education. Was the university encouraging pre-service and in-service teacher-learners to view their practices through lenses of social justice? Was it also providing adequate support for those people to bring their learning into reality in the field? Sandra posed valid and crucial questions. I'm not sure my nods and "hums" of support were enough, or even what she needed to hear. I just tried to listen so she might feel heard.

As I ruminated on my exchange with Sandra and began writing this chapter, I turned to other books for templates on what a final chapter might look, sound, and feel like. My first consultation was with Simpson's (2009) *Rediscovering Dewey*, both because of its overlapping content with this book around Dewey and because of my respect for Dr. Simpson's work.* Simpson frames the enormity of Dewey's democratic education (of which I consider social justice education an extension, if not a synonymous term) as a challenge for democratic or social justice educators:

> Progressive educators, however, have a significant problem. Most will think that Dewey's vision for democracy and communitarian individualism is admirable. They want to see it happen. Their problem is not that Dewey's vision of democracy is a bad idea; it is whether his vision of *the education for democracy* might be realistic....The bigger question, even if an educator is willing to put in all the work to educate for democracy, is whether it will make any difference (pp. 165-166).

Simpson goes on to affirm Dewey and those who continue to work in the vein of progressive education, suggesting that while the road is long and difficult, the aims are deeply worthy, even if never fully achieved. As I reviewed Simpson's positioning, I noted a quotation from Dewey (1937/1996) that I had underlined in my first reading of the book:

> If a sufficient number of educators devote themselves to striving courageously and with full sincerity to find the answers to the concrete questions which the idea and the aim put to us, I believe that the question of the relation of the schools to direction of social

---

* Full disclosure: Steven Simpson is both a publisher and editor of this book though he had no specific influence over my choice to cite his work.

change will cease to be a question, and will become a moving answer
in action (p. 418).

Two points of significance emerge from this passage in specific
connection to Sandra's story. First is Dewey's acknowledgment of
the courage educators demonstrate through their social justice
commitments; educators like Sandra and all of the educators whose
stories fill these pages. Maintaining that courage over a long time,
while full of reward, can be exhausting. As a movement, social justice
education must recognize there may be limits on individual teachers'
capabilities to maintain that required courage over time, especially for
those working in contexts where there is not clear and present support
for the advancement of social justice principles as a central part of
education. My assertion here affirms an immediate need to develop
the broadest possible networks of social justice educators to maximize
support and load-sharing to foster anti-oppressive conditions.
Participants in this **wide net** approach can include teachers, local and
regional administrators, parents, community members, and students.
The success of such a network is highly dependent on building
partnerships between those who identify as social justice educators and
other mainstream education stakeholders who are sympathetic to the
aims of social justice education (O'Sullivan, 2013). This proposal links
closely to the two purposes of this book outlined in the introduction:
a source of refueling for educators already engaged in social justice
work and an invitation for mainstream teachers to find opportunities
to bring aspects of social justice into their practice, even if their core
teacher identity isn't shaped around social justice. Forging alliances in
this way casts a wider net to support long-term enactment of social
justice practices.

A second related note of significance pertains to Dewey's words "a
moving answer in action." This turn of phrase emphasizes that social
justice education does not suggest a fixed destination but rather an
ongoing process driven by incremental actions that bring social justice
principles to life. In one sense, this suggestion of all journey and no
destination may feel disheartening for already overburdened social
justice educators. When connected with the above call for a wide net
approach, however, it may signify the possibility for educators to slow
their pace and focus on their practice, knowing others are taking up
the cause of social and ecological justice in their own ways, and no one
teacher or small group of educators need bear the weight of carrying

social justice education alone across any kind of predetermined finish line. A caveat to this way of thinking about social justice education practices is the need for frequent celebration of even the smallest achievements of social justice within any given segment of the network. These positive recognitions depend on network-locals to keep an eye on others' practices and to pause long enough to recognize the good work they are doing, even in small ways. Efforts to help social justice educators notice the good outcomes of their work catalyze hope and foster the courage needed to continue practices that support social justice. I hope this assessment offers hope to Sandra and others who endlessly forward social justice aims through their teaching.

The need for a wide net approach to social justice education, as well as dynamic, process-focused practices acknowledging even small social justice wins, is supported by the stories and activities shared throughout this book. In the following section, I briefly outline some trends and patterns threaded among all the stories, which respond to the ongoing refinement of what social justice looks, sounds, and feels like for teachers and students who are its practitioners.

TRENDS AND PATTERNS ACROSS ENVIRONMENTS, IDEAS, AND ACTIONS

Looking back on the stories in the previous three chapters, at least two patterns or trends appear to me:

- Recognition of **the moment** when an educator decides his or her commitment to a given social justice issue or situation is more important than the professional consequences that may result from pursuing or calling critical attention to that issue.

- **The importance of curricula** as a supportive and driving force in the ongoing implementation of social justice education.

The Moment

Many of the educator-storytellers acknowledge recognizing a moment in which they affirmed commitment to an element of social justice education even though following that path had actual or perceived negative professional consequences. Some of the teachers expressed this directly, while others made indirect statements. For instance, both Andrea and Mindy remarked in their respective stories that there came a time when they felt pursuing social justice work with their students (Andrea's pink shirt day and Mindy's production of *The Laramie Project*) was the right thing to do. This congruency may be an important indicator, an affirmation, of Dewey's "striving courageously." It is important to note that while Andrea identified explicitly as a strongly progressive social justice educator, Mindy did not readily assume such a professional identity, although she expressed support for many of the aims of social justice. I surmise that the underlying ethics of the moment can be a linking factor in the wide net approach to social justice education because while educators with social justice commitments may occupy many different positions on the political continuum from mainstream to radical, there is potential to find shared ground about "the right thing to do" where a given social justice issue is concerned.

Praxis Point ✍ Can you recall a moment in your own personal or professional life when you decided a social justice commitment was so important it was worth pursuing, even at some cost? This could be a significant undertaking like Andrea's day of action or Mindy's theatre production. It could also be a more everyday happening such as interrupting an intended lesson plan to inquire into a timely social justice issue as an impromptu learning moment.

    Going forward, try to take note of these moments when you encounter them, and make time where you can for reflecting on them, perhaps in a social justice journal.

The Importance of Curriculum

Many of the educator-storytellers shared about the importance of curriculum in supporting the work of social justice education. Curricula comes in many forms, including the official curriculum that is mandated by jurisdictional school authorities. Supplemental curricula can also be used in the service of specific social justice issues (i.e., the Project WILD program within environmental education or the Fly Kites Not Drones materials cited in *The Kite Runner* lesson plan in chapter four). As in recognizing the moment, this trend is identifiable both directly and also indirectly across the stories. Indirect examples include Zoe's inclusion of subversive literature to meet standard English curriculum expectations and Grace's mention of a supplemental curriculum program called EcoSchools,* while Andrea quite directly discussed the value of mining curricula for social justice outcomes.

Curriculum, particularly in its official form, acts as a backbone for contemporary schooling and, as such, is very important to the practice of social justice education in schools. Many social justice teachers identify curriculum as something of a double-edged sword. On one hand, curriculum is often over-packed, demanding quick coverage of many items and hindering deep analysis of any few items. The educators who I spoke to in preparing this book noted that curriculum often centres around lower-level, descriptive kinds of knowledge, rather than higher-order thinking that is needed to further social justice aims. On the other hand, mandated curriculum is often written in open-ended or non-prescriptive ways allowing social justice concerns to become a vehicle for achieving required curriculum expectations. O'Sullivan (2013), in regards to a particular public school's approach to social justice teaching, notes: "The teachers are busy delivering curriculum but, at times, delivering it with a difference" (p. 183). The nature of this difference will be different in every context. O'Sullivan points out that attempts to standardize or upscale specific curriculum approaches to social justice education are bound to fall flat if design changes aren't made to meet the needs of the new context.

Praxis Point ✍ Consider the curricula that shapes your interactions with students (again, this might include mandated curriculum, supplemental programs, or even curriculum designed by you as a teacher). Set aside some time to conduct a point-by-point review of your curricula (or, even some part of it). What opportunities does your curriculum present for taking up issues and topics of social justice that would be of interest and concern for the learners you teach?

---

* While the EcoSchool certification program isn't strictly speaking a curriculum, Grace's use of the program within her Green Team program is certainly a curricular application.

> **Tip:** Social justice education is at its best when it comes in the form of invitations and responses between educators and learners as opposed to soap box issues championed by the teacher without concern for students' interests. One strategy for navigating this is to search curricula for the broadest possible openings for taking up social justice and offer students choices around how they may want to respond within the broad window of social justice. This advice doesn't preclude ever introducing students to specific issues—indeed, some students might never learn about a particular issue without the teacher's prompt. Rather, the suggestion here is for teachers to seek attunement with social justice issues that are important to students and leverage curriculum to encourage their exploration of those issues.

FURTHER QUESTIONS AND NEW DIRECTIONS

In the introduction, I described this Outroductory chapter as a place of new beginnings from which people can move on rather than a source of conclusions. This is in no small part because social justice and social justice education are strongly process driven. Of course, there must be action, and there must be celebration of achievements. But, the doing of social justice is most importantly a way of being that is independent of any specific battles fought or campaigns won. With this in mind, I offer some points of focus for moving forward from this text. These are items that have continued to poke at my curiosity since having conducted the interviews and analyzed the stories shared by participants.

Social Justice Teacher Identity

In part one of the book, I wrote about ways social justice principles might be integrated into the personal and professional identity of teachers through the pedagogical choices they make in their practices. In part two, social justice educators' stories exemplified how their own ideas about social justice permeate their identities as educators. It is clear through the stories told in this research that how educators view themselves as teachers is influential in the ways social justice education is taken up in daily classroom practice. Still, understanding identity is a complex terrain and more work must be done to map this geography, both for the purpose of theoretical understandings and for the frontline practice of social justice education. Further enquiry may provide valuable insight into how social justice teacher identity begins and can be developed. This relates closely to the next point of need for more future research that transcends the experiences of individual teachers and explores the nature of broader networks and support structures that advance the development of social justice education as a movement.

Sustaining and Strengthening the Wide Net of Social Justice Education

The mainstay of the stories told throughout this book, and the majority of social justice education initiatives conducted (at least in public schools) involve a lone teacher or small cadres of educators operating without significant systemic support (Campigotto & Barrett, in press). Perhaps the most important ongoing work needed to foster social justice education is the fertilization of interconnected networks (the wide net) to support educators and learners who are working together in the interests of equity, challenging privilege and oppression, building community, and fostering agency and action.

The emergence of strong networks could ease some of the difficulties individual social justice educators describe. While networks have the capacity to enable sharing of resources and strategies for social justice education, this is not the primary need they fulfill. More important is their capacity to offer teachers support and ongoing reassurance that social justice principles are central and valuable parts of what it means to be an educator or learner, and to be in the ongoing process of being educated. This stands in opposition to the ideas social justice educators often report facing: that social justice is fringe, extracurricular, or somehow falls outside the main purposes of education. I have a notion that more robust networks of educators and support personnel, within and outside public education, could normalize social justice education and ease the burden of justifying or defending its importance in teaching and learning. More research, both theorizing and empirical analysis, is needed to test this hunch.

RISING TO THE CHALLENGE

In the opening paragraph of the book, I described education, especially social justice education, as a messy business. The story of my conversation with Sandra is an illustration of the discomfort that can come from navigating this messiness every day as a teacher. It is also an effective story to springboard into an outroduction of the challenges social justice educators describe throughout the book. The need for ongoing work to address these challenges must be taken up jointly by social justice teachers at all levels, including and especially academics like myself. Academics have time in our job routines to research and advocate for policy changes on behalf of frontline educators whose work lives are more than filled up with the everyday doing of social justice education.

I don't want to end this book on the idea that social justice education is all challenge and no achievement. Social justice educators all around the world (who use many names to describe their work) are working hard and making a difference that little by little (or sometimes by leaps and bounds) forwards social justice aims. As an example of these impacts, I return to my friend Sandra. The earlier snapshot of my conversation with Sandra highlights a reasonable moment of despair without reference to the strength, resilience, and hopefulness with which Sandra champions social justice education every day in her classroom. For example, she leads an extracurricular "outers club," introducing young people to their local environment through outdoor adventure activities. She teaches directly about social justice issues like racism, poverty, sexism, and homophobia through her curriculum delivery, especially through language and math. And, in a bigger picture way, all of her pedagogical choices are filtered through a lens, recognizing the social context in which she teaches as one of mixed socio-economic status, where some students' families are relatively wealthy while others may have trouble meeting basic needs.

In the second part of chapter one, I provided a list of six practice points for social justice educators. Though I stated explicitly that it wasn't intended as a checklist of all the right things to do as a social justice educator, one could probably hold such a list up to Sandra's teaching practice and see many of those actions and dispositions at work. This is also true of the educators whose stories I was gifted to share in part two. My purpose in showcasing any of these teachers is not to valourize their work—they, like Sandra, are extraordinary educators doing, for the most part, ordinary things in well designed and intentional ways. And their work is hard work. The tips, strategies, or stories offered in this book are meant to make social justice education more accessible and appealing, but it is still hard work. In the face of this, social justice educators rise to the challenge. Their commitment is evidenced in their stories, and for me, their stories (of success, failure, and in between) demonstrate the moral value of social justice. I hope their stories as well as the activities and strategies shared here inspire similar commitments to social justice for readers. And that those commitments find outlets in teaching practices that will generate more stories. I look forward to hearing them.

ACKNOWLEDGEMENTS

Much like social justice work, writing a book takes a community. I am grateful for the support of family, friends and colleagues who have helped and encouraged me in this project from start to finish.

Family: Mom and Alan, Dad and Marion, Jamie, Lauren, Tricia, and Lori: Thank you for your support over the long haul. Clayton, thanks for helping me see the world anew in the last leg of this current journey.

Friends and colleagues who continue to shape my thinking about education, social justice, and writing: Gerald Walton, Leigh Potvin, Bob Jickling, Mary Breunig, Paul Berger, Connie Russell, Emily Root, Greg Lowan-Trudeau, Pat Maher, Deborah Berrill, Karleen Pendleton Jimenez, Cathy Bruce, Jackie Muldoon, Rachael Nicholls, Denise Handlarski, Lisa Mitchell, Kathy Haras, Brian Lisson, Natalie Gillis, & Robert Powell.

The partners at Wood N Barnes for their belief in this book and my ability to write it.

RESOURCES FOR SOCIAL JUSTICE EDUCATORS

These national and international organizations may be helpful in supporting educators who are interested in social justice across a broad range of issues related to the elements of environments, ideas, and actions explained in chapter two and across chapters three, four, and five.

Resources are arranged according to the elements of environments, ideas, and actions. As noted in the book, these concepts are linked in complex ways. Likewise, the organizations that support social justice education cannot be easily divided or compartmentalized. I have organized based purely on my own understanding of the main work of each organization.

Of course, this list is not exhaustive; readers can draw support and inspiration from many other regional, national, and international organizations and networks.

ENVIRONMENTS

Association for Experiential Education
Website: aee.org
AEE is an international organization committed to supporting educators in implementing opportunities for experiential education in a range of educational contexts from schools to community and popular education, to outdoor and adventure learning. An international conference is held each year, typically in the late fall. Regional conferences and events are held throughout the year.

International Alliance for Invitational Education
Website: invitationaleducation.net
IAIE is a global organization which, according to their website, is "dedicated to the development of positive school, work, and home environments as well as opposed to those forces that demean and defeat human potential." In addition to an annual conference, IAIE also offers many publications that support their organizational aims of more inviting educational environments.

My GSA (by Equality for Gays and Lesbians Everywhere)
Website: mygsa.ca
This site, hosted by EGALE Canada, provides teachers and students who wish to organize a Gay/Straight Alliance group with a resource kit for getting started. The kit offers information and strategies that may

be especially useful for educators who are new to supporting a G/SA, or in instances where school administration or community members need information about what a G/SA is, and how it can be a tool for creating a safe school environment for LGBTQ youth and their allies.

Preparing Youth to Thrive
Website: selpractices.org
This comprehensive report "guidebook" presents a framework for integrating social and emotional learning approaches into a variety of learning contexts. The framework is designed around wise practices in seven aspects of social-emotional learning: Emotion management, empathy, teamwork, responsibility, initiative, and problem-solving. Case narratives, notes on student experience, and staff practices offer guideposts for implementing quality social-emotional learning.

Roots of Empathy
Website: rootsofempathy.org
Roots of Empathy is an international program offering weekly facilitated visits of a baby and parent into elementary school classrooms. Each week students interact with the infant and track its development over the school year. The baby serves as a living object-lesson (or, a subject-lesson, in this case), through which youth can think about empathy and other concepts of social-emotional learning. The program is strongly evidence-based, and shows results in reducing children's demonstration of aggressive behaviour.

IDEAS

The Action Research Network of the Americas
Website: arnawebsite.org
ARNA integrates and supports scholars and practitioners (and their participants, students, clients, etc.) in education, healthcare, and other disciplines to engage in research to improve practice. Theoretical frameworks for action research are frequently aligned with the goals of social justice; indeed, action research may best be described as research conducted by the people, and for the people. ARNA holds an annual conference in the late spring.

Avaaz.org
Website: aavez.org
AVAAZ is a web-based knowledge-mobilization tool for a broad range of issues related to democracy and social justice. In their own words,

"Avaaz is a global web movement to bring people-powered politics to decision-making everywhere." The organizers use online petitions and crowdfunding to raise awareness and money to support social justice initiatives. Avaaz claims victories in campaigns related to climate change and environmental (in)justice, corporate power (in)justice, government corruption and reform, and many more.

Canadian Centre for Policy Alternatives
Website: policyalternatives.ca/
This policy "think-tank" develops reports and publications related to a range of social justice issues. For instance, CCPA produces an annual "alternative federal budget" that demonstrates how social justice (and other) priorities could be accomplished if the Government of Canada constructed the country's budget differently. Also, CCPA publishes Our Schools, Our Selves, a popular journal that serves as "a lively, accessible forum for debates and discussion on topics such as Indigenous education, anti-racism classroom programs, sex education, commercialism, child care, and much more." While this is a Canadian organization, some of their policy analyses may be useful for social justice educators and champions in other countries.

Human Rights Watch
Website: hrw.org
This investigative "watchdog" group prepares reports that raise awareness and spur action to end human rights abuses in 90 countries around the world. HRW functions independently of any government or political party. In addition to many excellent resources on human rights abuses in specific regional contexts, the video series "Human Rights 101" is an excellent resource for social justice educators and their students/participants.

TakingITGlobal
Website: tigweb.org
Through its online presence, and face-to-face workshops, TIG provides a forum for digital youth engagement, global education, and social innovation. Described on their website as "a social network for social good," TIG connects global youth animators and activists who are interested in social justice issues.

ACTIONS

Black Lives Matter

Website: blacklivesmatter.com

Few contemporary social justice movements are more radical in their approach to nonviolent social justice action than Black Lives Matter. With chapters across the United States and Canada, BLM represents a grassroots movement to demand an end to systemic racial oppression experienced by Black people, especially (but not exclusively) where interactions with police are concerned. Many educators may feel uncomfortable using BLM as a resource in schools because of the level of controversy that surrounds the group. However, the guiding principles described on BLM's website could be a good starting point for discussing the movement's aims. Consider comparing BLM's principles with other frameworks of social justice education, such as the principles that I introduce in chapters one and two.

Canadian Centre for Gender and Sexual Diversity

Website: ccgsd-ccdgs.org/

Among its many programs, CCGSD is a champion of the Day of Pink event described by Andrea in chapter five. Their mission is to "support and transform Canadian and indigenous communities from coast to coast to coast in a shared vision of a discrimination-free gender and sexually diverse world." They enact this mission through a range of programming including forums and conferences for educators and youth across Canada.

Idle No More

Website: idlenomore.ca

Idle No More challenges the legacy of colonialism that continues to oppress Indigenous Peoples. While there is a strong focus on colonialism in the Canadian context,

Rethinking Schools

Website: rethinkingschools.org

Beginning with their popular magazine of the same title, Rethinking Schools has grown into a significant publisher of educational materials that support social justice. The organization is exemplary of the kind of praxis (reflective thinking in action) advocated by social justice theorist and activist Paulo Freire. Check out their teacher planbook (Planning to Change the World) designed specifically with social justice educators in mind.

WE.org

Website: we.org

WE.org is a family of organizations that foster an ethic of globality through leadership development, activism, and social enterprise. "WE Day" events are youth activist and leadership conventions that can be attended around the world by young people who demonstrate a commitment to social change making.

350.org

Website: 350.org

With a specific focus on climate justice, 350.org brings people together to "oppose new coal, oil and gas projects, take money out of the companies that are heating up the planet, and build 100% clean energy solutions that work for all." 350.org is known for using innovative mass public actions where everyday people demonstrate their commitment to maintaining a world in which carbon dioxide levels remain at or below 350 parts per million. On their website, 350.org offers useful resources for explaining climate science in plain language, as well as strategies and inspiration for sparking local action to curb climate change.

REFERENCES

Abdi, A. A. (2013). Recontextualizing and reculturing education for "democratic" consciousness: Social and philosophical analysis. In A. A. Abdi & P. R. Carr (Eds.), *Educating for democratic consciousness: Counter-hegemonic possibilities* (pp. 14-28). New York: Peter Lang.

Abram, D. (1997). *The spell of the sensuous: Perception and language in a more-than-human world.* New York: Vintage Books.

Al Jezeera English. (2007, May 20). *Afghanistan – The toughest battle – Kite running – 14 May 07* [Video file]. Retrieved from: https://www.youtube.com/watch?v=i5S47aSlezs

Ambreen, T. & Berger, E. (2016). To diversify the outdoors, we have to think about who we're excluding. *Outside Magazine.* Retrived from: https://www.outsideonline.com/2131911/diversify-outdoors-we-have-to-think-about-who-were-excluding

Apple, M., Gandin, L. A., & Hypolito, A. M. (2001). Paulo Freire. In J. A. Palmer (Ed.), *Fifty modern thinkers on education: From Piaget to the present.* (pp. 128-132). New York: Routledge.

Apple, M, & Teitelbaum, K. (2002). John Dewey. In J. A. Palmer (Ed.), *Fifty major thinkers on education: From Confucius to Dewey.* (pp. 177-181). New York: Routledge.

Bashir, N. Y., Lockwood, P., Chasteen, A. L., Nadolny, D., & Noyes, I. (2013). The ironic impact of activists: Negative stereotypes reduce social change influence. *European Journal of Social Psychology, 43(7),* 614-626.

Beal, C., Mason Bolick, C. M., & Martorella, P. H. (2009). *Teaching social studies in middle and secondary school (5th Ed.).* Upper Saddle River, NJ: Pearson.

Bell, N. (2014). Teaching by the Medicine Wheel: An Anishnaabe framework for Indigenous education. *Education Canada, 54(3).* Retrieved from: http://www.cea-ace.ca/education-canada/article/teaching-medicine-wheel

Blenkensop, S. (2012). Four slogans for cultural change: An evolving place-based, imaginative, and ecological learning experience. *Journal of Moral Education, 41(3),* 353-368.

Blenkensop, S. (2014). In search of the eco-teacher: Public school edition. *Canadian Journal of Environmental Education, 19,* 145-159.

Boaler, J. (2016). *Mathematical mindsets: Unleashing students' potential through creative math, inspiring messages and innovative teaching.* San Francisco: Jossey Bass.

Breunig, M. C. (2005). Turning experiential education and critical pedagogy theory into praxis. *Journal of Experiential Education, 28(2),* 106-122.

Cain, J., & Jolliff, B. (1998). *Teamwork and teamplay.* Dubuque, IA: Kendall/Hunt.

Campigotto, R., & Barrett, S. (in press). Addressing the challenges of being a teacher activist: A phenomenological study of pre-service teachers who are passionate about environmental education. *Canadian Journal of Environmental Education.*

Carr, P. (2011). The quest for a critical pedagogy of democracy: In: C. Stephenson Mallot & B. Porfilio (Eds.), *Critical pedagogy in the twenty-first century: A new generaton of scholars* (pp. 187-212). Charlotte, NC: Information Age. [Adobe Digital Editions]

Carr, P. (2011b). *Does your vote count? Critical pedagogy and democracy.* New York: Peter Lang.

Carr, P. (2013). Reshaping the democratic truth, and rethinking democracy without elections. In A. A. Abdi, & P. Carr (Eds.), *Educating for democratic consciousness: Counter-hegemonic possibilities* (pp. 29-49). New York: Peter Lang.

Carson, R. (1965/1998). *The sense of wonder.* New York: HarperCollins.

Checkoway, B. (2011). What is youth participation? *Children and Youth Services Review, 33,* 340-345.

Chomsky, N. (2000). *Chomsky on miseducation.* Lanham, MD: Rowman and Littlefield.

Cribb, A. & Gewirtz, S. (2003). Towards a sociology of just practices: An analysis of plural conceptions of justice. In C. Vincent (Ed.), *Social justice, education and identity.* (pp. 15-30). New York: RoutledgeFalmer.

Darder, A. (2002). *Reinventing Freire: A pedagogy of love.* Boulder, CO: Westview Press.

Darder, A. (2009). Teaching as an act of love: Reflections on Paulo Freire and his contribution to our lives and work. In A. Darder, M. P. Baltodano, & R. D. Torres (Eds.), *The critical pedagogy reader, 2nd Ed.* (pp. 567-578). New York: Routledge.

Dewey, J. (1897). My pedagogic creed. In J. A. Boydson (Ed.), *The early works of John Dewey, volume 5: 1895-1898* (pp. 84-93). Intelex. [Past Masters e-book]

Dewey, J. (1918). *Democracy and education.* New York: Macmillan.

Dewey, J. (1933). *How we think: A restatement of the relation of reflective thinking to the educative process.* Boston: D. C. Heath and Company.

Dewey, J. (1937/1996) Education and social change. In J. A. Boydston/L. Hickson (Eds.), *The later works of John Dewey, 1925-1953. Volume 11: 1935-1937, Essays, liberalism, and social action.* Charlottesville, VA: InteLex. [Past Masters electronic version]

Dewey, J. (1938). *Experience and education.* New York: Macmillan.

Doctorow, C. (2008). *Little brother.* New York: Tom Doherty Assoc.

Fawcett, L., Bell, A., & Russell, C. (2002). Guiding our environmental praxis: Teaching for social and environmental justice. In W. Leal Filho (Ed.), *Teaching sustainability at universities: Towards curriculum greening* (pp.223 – 228). New York: Peter Lang.

Fielding, A. & Barker, M. (2013). The innovators: Interview with Craig Morrison and Lauren Hortie, Oasis Skateboard Factory. Retrieved from: http://notesfromthefield.ca/talking-with-teachers-in-alternative-schools/oasis-skateboard-factory/

Fisher, R. G. (2000). *After the fire: A true story of love and survival.* New York: Little, Brown & Company.

Flores, A. (2007). Examining Disparities in Mathematics Education: Achievement Gap or Opportunity Gap? *The High School Journal, 91(1)*, 29–42. http://doi.org/10.1353/hsj.2007.0022

Forster, M. (Director). (2008). *The kite runner* [Motion picture]. United States: Participant productions.

Frank, L. (2013). *Journey toward the caring classroom, 2Ed.* Bethany, OK: Wood N Barnes Publishing.

Freire, P. (1985/2013). Reading the world and reading the word: An interview with Paulo Freire. In W. Hare & J. P. Portelli (Eds.), *Philosophy of Education: Introductory readings (4th Ed.)*. Calgary, AB: Brush Education. [Kindle Edition]

Freire, P. (1970). *Pedagogy of the oppressed* (M. Bergman Ramos, Trans.). New York: Continuum.

Freire, P. (1994). *Pedagogy of hope* (R. R. Barr, Trans.). London: Continuum. (Original work published 1992)

Gibson-Wood, H. & Wakefield, S. (2013). "Participation," white privilege, and environmental justice. *Antipode: A Radical Journal of Geography, 45(3)*, 641-662.

Giroux, H. (2004). *When hope is subversive*. Tikkun, 19(6), 38-39.

Giroux, H. (2009). Critical theory and educational practice. In A. Dardar, M. P. Baltadano, & R. D. Torres (Eds.), *The critical pedagogy reader* (pp. 27-51).

Haras, K. (2003). An exploration of meaningful involvement in ropes course programs (Doctoral dissertation). Retrieved from *Proquest Thesis and Dissertations*. (#3117490)

Haras, K., Bunting, C., & Witt, P. (2006). Meaningful involvement opportunities in ropes course programs. *Journal of Leisure Research, 38(3)*, 339-362.

HDNetWorldReport. (2011, January 15). *Viewfinder: The real kite runners* [Video file]. Retrieved from: https://www.youtube.com/watch?v=sfeNUaKxufA

Hedges, C. (2010). *Empire of illusion: The end of literacy and the triumph of spectacle*. New York: Knopf. [Kindle edition]

Hess, D. E. (2009). *Controversy in the classroom: The democratic power of discussion*. New York: Routledge.

Hewitt, V. M. (2001). Examining the Reggio Emilia approach to early childhood education. *Early Childhood Education Journal, 29(2)*, 95-100.

Hickman, L. (2012). Dewey, Democracy and Global Citizenship lecture. Ikeda Center for Peace, Learning and Dialogue. Retrieved from: http://www.ikedacenter.org/thinkers-themes/thinkers/lectures-talks/hickman-lecture

Hoffman, J., & Jones, K. (2001). Barefoot mapping. Available from http://sierraclub.bc.ca/wp-content/uploads/2015/08/Barefoot-Mapping_8-12.pdf

hooks, b. (1994). *Teaching to transgress*. New York: Routledge. [Kindle Edition]

hooks, b. (2004). *Teaching community: A pedagogy of hope*. New York: Routledge.

Hoover, R. (2013). Animating democracy: The civic and pedagogical imperatives. In A. A. Abdi & P. R. Carr (Eds.), *Educating for democratic consciousness: Counter-hegemonic possibilities* (pp. 123-135). New York: Peter Lang.

Hosseini, K. (2004). *The kite runner*. New York: Penguin Random House.

Jennings, L. B., Perra-Medina, D. M., Hilfinger-Messias, D. K., & McLoughlin, K. (2006). Towards a critical social theory of youth empowerment. *Journal of Community Practice, 14(1-2),* 31-55.

Jensen, D. (2004). *Walking on water: Reading, writing, and revolution.* White River Junction, VT: Chelsea Green.

Jickling, B. (2009). Sitting on an old grey stone: Meditations on emotional understanding. In M. McKenzie, H. Bai, P. Hart, & B. Jickling (Eds.), *Fields of Green: Restoring Culture, Environment, and Education* (pp. 163-173). Cresskill, NJ: Hampton Press.

Jickling, B., Lotz-Sisitka, H., O'Donoghue, R., & Ogbuigwe, A. (2006). *Environmental education, ethics, & action: A workbook to get started.* Hertfordshire, UK: United Nations Environment Program.

Keegan, R. (2012). *Global games for diversity education: New ways of learning in the 21ˢᵗ century.* Bethany, OK: Wood N Barnes Publishing.

Kemchandani-Daswani, S. (no date). *The kite runner companion curriculum.* Amnesty International Human Rights Education Program. https://www.amnestyusa.org/sites/default/files/kiterunnerhigh_0.pdf

Kincheloe, J. (2008). *Critical pedagogy (2nd ed.).* New York: Peter Lang.

Kirman, J. M. (2008). *Elementary social studies: Creative classroom ideas (4th Ed.).* Toronto: Pearson Education Canada.

Kumashiro, K. (2004). *Against common sense: Teaching and learning toward social justice.* New York: Routledge.

Lawson, A. (2007). Learning mathematics vs. following "rules": The value of student-generated methods. *What Works: Research into Practice, Research Monograph #2.* Toronto, ON: Ontario Literacy and Numeracy Secretariat. http://www.edu.gov.on.ca/eng/literacynumeracy/inspire/research/Lawson.pdf

Levin, J., Nolan, J. F., Kerr, J. W., & Elliot, A. E. (2012). *Principles of classroom management: A professional decision making model.* Toronto: Pearson.

McLaren, P. (2009). Critical pedagogy: A look at the major concepts. In A. Dardar, M. P. Baltadano, & R. D. Torres (Eds.), *The critical pedagogy reader* (pp. 61-84). New York: Routledge.

Mears, J. (2012, January/February). The many benefits of community mapping. *Connect, 1-5.*

Monchinski, T. (2011). *Engaged pedagogy, enraged pedagogy: Reconciling politics, emotion, religion, and science for critical pedagogy.*

Nieto, S. & Bode, P. (2012). *Affirming diversity: The sociopolitical context of multicultural education.*

Niblett, B. (in press). Facilitating activist education: Social and environmental justice in classroom practice to promote achievement, equity, and wellbeing. *What Works: Research into Practice, 67.*

Niblett, B., & Potvin, L. (2010). Exploring gender norms through the "colour blind" initiative. *Pathways: The Ontario Journal of Outdoor Education, 22(2),* 4-6.

Norgaard, K. M. (2012). Climate denial and the construction of innocence: Reproducing Transnational environmental privilege in the face of climate change. *Race, Gender & Class, 19(1/2),* 80-103.

Oakes, J., & Lipton, M. (1999). *Teaching to change the world*. Boston: McGraw-Hill College.

Oasis Skateboard Factory. (2016). Retrieved from: http://oasisskateboardfactory.blogspot.ca

Odhiambo, E. A., Nelson, L. E., Chrisman, K. (2016). *Social studies and young children*. Upper Saddle River, NJ: Pearson.

Orr, D. (2002). *The nature of design: Ecology, culture, and human intention*. New York, NY: Oxford University Press.

O'Sullivan, M. (2013). Challenging neoliberal anti-intellectualism, consumerism, and utilitarianism: Achieving Deweyian and Freirean visions of critically engaged citizens. In A. Abdi & P. R. Carr (Eds.), *Educating for democratic consciousness: counter-hegemonic possibilities* (pp. 167-186). New York: Peter Lang.

Our Journey To Smile. (2014, March 23). *Fly kites not drones in Afghanistan* [Video file].

Palmer, P. J. (2007). *The courage to teach: Exploring the inner landscape of a teacher's life (10th Anniv. Ed.)*. San Francisco: Josey-Bass.

People For Education. (2015). Ontario's schools: The gap between policy and reality: People For Education annual report on Ontario's publicly funded schools. Available from: http://www.peopleforeducation.ca/wp-content/uploads/2015/06/P4E-Annual-Report-2015.pdf

Piersol, L. (2014). Our hearts leap up: Awaking wonder within the classroom. In K. Egan, A. I. Cant, & G. Judson (Eds.), *Wonder-full education: The centrality of wonder in teaching and learning across the curriculum* (pp. 3-21). New York: Routledge.

Purkey, W. W. & Novak, J. M. (2008). *Fundamentals of invitational education*. Kennesaw, GA: The International Alliance for Invitational Education.

Rainforest Foundation UK. (2011). *Mapping for rights: Participatory mapping*. Available from http://www.mappingforrights.org/participatory_mapping

Richter, R., & Molomot, L. (2013). *School's out: Lessons from a forest kindergarten* [Motion picture]. United States: Linden Tree Films.

Rifkin, J. (2009). *The empathic civilization*. New York: Penguin. [Kobo Edition].

Russell, C. (2014). *Spending my privilege: University teaching, research, and administration for social justice and environmental sustainability*. Retrieved from: http://www.placecentre.org/connie-russell.html

Sagan, C. (2001). Wonder and skepticism. In W. Hare & J. P. Portelli (Eds.), *Philosophy of education: Introductory readings* (pp. 157-166). Calgary: Detselig.

Sapon-Shevin, M. (2007). *Widening the circle: The power of inclusive classrooms*. Boston: Beacon.

Schugurensky, D. (2013). Democracy does not fall from the sky. In A. Abdi & P. R. Carr (Eds.), *Educating for democratic consciousness: counter-hegemonic possibilities* (pp. ix-xii). New York: Peter Lang.

Sensoy, O., & DiAngello, R. (2012). *Is everyone really equal? An introduction to key concepts in social justice education*. New York: Teacher's College Press.

Simpson, S. (2011). *Rediscovering Dewey: A reflection on independent thinking*. Bethany, OK: Wood N Barnes Publishing.

Smith, J., Down, B., & McInerney, P. (2014). *The socially just school: making space for youth to speak back.* Dordrecht, Germany: Springer.

Smith, T. E., Knapp, C. E., Seaman, J, & Pace, S. (2011). Experiential education and learning by experience. In T. E. Smith & C. E. Knapp (Eds.), *Sourcebook of Experiential Education* (pp. 1-12). New York: Routledge.

Stanchfield, J. (2014). Inspired educator, inspired learner: Experiential, brain-based activities and strategies to engage, motivate, build community, and create lasting lessons. Bethany OK: Wood N Barnes Publishing.

Stavros, J. & Torres, C. (2005). *Dynamic relationships: Unleashing the power of appreciative inquiry in daily living.* Chagrin Falls, OH: Taos Institute Publications.

Stinson, D. W. (2004). Mathematics as "gate-keeper": Three theoretical perspectives that aim toward empowering all children with a key to the gate. *The Mathematics Educator, 14(1),* 8–18. Available at: http://math.coe.uga.edu/tme/Issues/v14n1/v14n1.Stinson.pdf Also available at: http://digitalarchive.gsu.edu/msit_facpub/19/

Stires, A. (2016). A winter day in the life: An east coast nature preschool and forest kindergarten. In D. Sobel (Ed.), *Nature preschools and forest kindergartens: The handbook for outdoor learning.* St. Paul, MN: Readleaf Press. [Kindle Edition]

Stocker, D. (2006). *Math that matters: A teacher resource linking math and social justice.* Canadian Centre for Policy Alternatives, www.policyalternatives.ca/offices/national

Stocker, D., & Wagner, D. (2007). Talking about teaching mathematics for social justice. *For the Learning of Mathematics, 27(3),* 17–21.

Tupper, J. (2007). From care-less to care-full education for citizenship in schools and beyond. *Alberta Journal of Educational Research, 53(3),* 259-272.

Watkins, C. (2012). *Learners in the driving seat.* School Leadership Today, 1(2), 28-31.

Weiler, K. (2003). Paulo Freire: On hope. *Radical Teacher, 67,* 32-35.

Weston, A. (2008). *A rulebook for arguments, 4th Ed.* Indianapolis, IN: Hackett Publishing Company.

Wink, J. (2011). *Critical pedagogy: Notes from the real world.* Upper Saddle River, NJ: Pearson.

Young, I. M. (1990). *Justice and the politics of difference.* Princeton, NJ: Princeton University Press.

Zyngier, D. (2008). (Re)conceptualizing student engagement: Doing education not doing time. *Teaching and Teacher Education, 24,* 1765-1776.

Blair Niblett, Ph.D., is an assistant professor at Trent University's School of Education and Professional Learning, where he designs hands-on experiences to illustrate theoretical concepts both in and out of the classroom. His research explores the intersections of broadly defined concepts of social justice and experiential education. He studied outdoor recreation and education at Lakehead University and continues to be active as a senior consultant and challenge course trainer with Adventureworks! Associates Inc. He lives in Toronto, Canada with his paddleboard and his bikes.